HOW
YOUR IRA
CAN MAKE
YOU A
MILLIONAIRE

HOW YOUR IRA CAN MAKE YOU A MILLIONAIRE

ARNOLD CORRIGAN

HARMONY BOOKS

New York

To Paul and Ethan, without whose encouragement this book would not have been conceived, or started, or finished.

Copyright © 1983 by Arnold Corrigan

Published by Harmony Books, a division of Crown Publishers, Inc., One Park Avenue, New York, New York 10016 and simultaneously in Canada by General Publishing Company Limited

HARMONY BOOKS and colophon are trademarks of Crown Publishers, Inc. Manufactured in the United States of America

Library of Congress Cataloging in Publication Data

Corrigan, Arnold.
　How your IRA can make you a millionaire.

　1.　Individual retirement accounts.　I.　Title.
HG1660.A3C6　1982　　　331.25'2　　82-15483

ISBN: 0-517-54917-4 (cloth)
　　　0-517-54918-2 (paper)

10 9 8 7 6 5 4 3

First Edition

CONTENTS

TABLES

ACKNOWLEDGMENTS

I wish particularly to thank Sam D'Agostino for his thoughtful comments on the manuscript, and Richard L. Keschner, Esq., whose inexhaustible knowledge of retirement-plan tax law saved me from innumerable errors. Any remaining errors are, of course, completely my own.

INTRODUCTION: WHY YOU SHOULD OPEN AN IRA

Can an IRA make you a millionaire? Yes. Will it? Maybe. It's up to you. This book will show that the possibilities of an Individual Retirement Account—*IRA* for short—are tremendous. But just how successful your own IRA will be depends very much on how you *manage* your IRA—how well you take advantage of the choices that the law allows.

Some people will manage better, some worse. There will be an extraordinary difference in dollars between good management and careless management. Some people really will end up as millionaires. And a surprising number, whether they reach that figure or not, will find that the IRA has been their key to a rich retirement.

This book is for everyone who has started an IRA or is thinking of starting one. It will help you manage your IRA in a way that will suit you best and that will do the most for your financial future. It will suggest the best investments for your IRA and will help you fit the IRA into your total financial planning.

First, just what is an IRA? It is that rarest of creations—a government tax program that actually helps you. In an unprecedented break for savers, the Economic Recovery Tax Act of 1981 took the existing IRA concept and eliminated many of its restrictions; it opened up IRAs to everyone who works for a living and is trying to save for retirement.

Anyone with earned income can now put up to $2,000 a year into an IRA—whether or not you are also covered by a company or government retirement plan. The full amount you contribute is taken as a deduction on your federal income tax return.

Does the law really benefit everyone? Not exactly. If you can't accumulate savings, the IRA won't help you. And it's true that many people find themselves unable to save.

But if you can save, the IRA offers you a double tax advantage that can make a real difference over the years. Not only are your *contributions tax-deductible,* but your money *earns and compounds tax-free* until you withdraw the savings at retirement. You may have seen tables showing the great benefits of tax-free compounding and wondered if the benefits were real. Yes, they are real—the advantage of tax-free compounding is tremendous. Just how the figures work out over twenty or thirty years is something we will look at in chapter 8.

With the double tax advantage, the IRA cuts through the two problems that have made it difficult to build up savings successfully. In the past, whatever savings you could put aside had to be taken from after-tax income, without any help from the tax laws. Then, except for a very small exclusion, any interest or dividends earned on these savings were fully taxable, cutting down the compounding effect. Tax shelters that helped get around these problems were usually not practical for the average person.

When the IRA was first introduced in 1975, it was only for individuals who were not covered under any other retirement plan. Contributions were limited to 15 percent of earned income and were subject to a flat ceiling of $1,500 annually. While several million IRAs were opened between 1975 and 1981, the IRA fell far short of the near-universal savings plan that it has become under the new law. The 1982 changes are dramatic; for the first time, people of moderate income have a broad, practical tax shelter of their own.

Now that the IRA is available to almost everyone, should *you* open an IRA? The answer is likely to be yes. Even if you are covered by a company retirement plan and by Social Security, you probably suspect that your retirement won't be as comfortable as it's supposed to be. Perhaps your company plan looks generous— but what happens if you leave the company or if it goes out of business? You should be well aware of how you would come out in these cases. As for Social Security, the nation's economic problems have caused this once-great trust fund to shrink; there's a considerable possibility that benefits in the future will be less favorable than in the past. It will be to your advantage to have additional funds set aside in your IRA.

And then there's inflation—which wasn't always the problem it is now for those saving for retirement. In the 1950s, the cost of living in the United States rose by an average of only 2 percent annually, and in the 1960s by 3 percent. But the inflation rate rose to over 12 percent in 1979 and 1980 and is still in the 6 to 8 percent range in 1982. Even if the rate drops, it's not likely to get back to the low levels of twenty years ago.

There is no way of predicting whether the future benefits in your company plan and in Social Security will be indexed adequately to inflation. But the IRA provides two kinds of protection against inflation. First, it lets you set aside a large additional amount for retirement. Second, you can choose investments for your IRA that will grow with inflation, creating what professional investors term an *inflation hedge*.

Before we go on to the crucial question of selecting your IRA investments, let's review some of the key facts about IRAs.

WHO IS ELIGIBLE?

As pointed out above, everyone with *earned income* is eligible to start an IRA. Even if you are already covered by a corporate or government retirement plan or by a Keogh plan, you can still have an IRA. Self-employed persons no longer have to choose between a Keogh plan and an IRA; they can have both. All earned income qualifies—any income for services rendered—whether it be wages, salaries, bonuses, commissions, tips, etc. But if your only income was from dividends, interest, rents, royalties, or a pension, these are not considered earned income, and they don't qualify. Another limitation: there's an upper age limit of seventy and a half for contributions (you cannot start an IRA or contribute to an IRA in the tax year in which you reach age seventy and a half, or in subsequent years). On the other hand, there's no lower age limit. The teenager who earns $2,000 in a year has the right to put all of it in an IRA; the immediate tax benefit may be slight, but having the money in a tax-free fund could be highly profitable later on.

HOW MUCH CAN I CONTRIBUTE?

You can contribute up to $2,000 annually, but not *more* than your total earned income. (If your earned income is $1,000, you can only contribute $1,000.)

WHAT'S THE PERCENTAGE LIMIT?

There isn't any. Before 1982, contributions to an IRA were limited to 15 percent of earned income. Now you can contribute any percentage of your earned income up to $2,000.

Of course, for the low-income person who earns only $8,000 to $10,000 a year, the opportunity to put up to $2,000 into an IRA may not have much practical meaning. But consider, for example, the spouse who works part-time and earns $4,000 a year, not all of which needs to be spent currently. The limit on his or her IRA contribution before 1982 was 15 percent of $4,000, or only $600. Now up to $2,000 can go into an IRA.

WHEN DO I MAKE MY CONTRIBUTION?

You can open your IRA and contribute at any time during the year and up to the time your income tax return is due—normally April 15. If you have obtained an extension for filing your tax return, then you can contribute until the date of the extension. Contributions can be made in a lump sum or in installments. In order to get the maximum benefit from the tax-free compounding of the earnings on your contributions, you should make your contribution as early in the year as possible.

CAN I CONTRIBUTE LESS THAN $2,000?

Certainly. The law does not set any minimum. You can vary your contribution within the limit, or skip a year completely. (As we shall see, most individual sponsors do set minimums, but there are enough choices available so that this should not be a problem.) The point to remember is that any part of the tax deduction not used in a given year is permanently lost; you can't make up the contribution in a following year.

HOW DO I TAKE THE TAX DEDUCTION?

You can deduct your IRA contribution on your federal income tax return even if you do not itemize other deductions. Before 1982 the IRA deduction could only be taken on Form 1040 (the standard long form), but the IRS had indicated that beginning in 1982 there will also be a space for the IRA deduction on Form 1040A (the short form).

WHAT IF BOTH SPOUSES WORK?

If both spouses have earned income, each is eligible for a completely separate IRA, and each can contribute up to $2,000 (if earned income equals or exceeds that amount), so that the combined deduction could be as high as $4,000. The couple can file either a joint or separate tax returns.

WHAT IF ONE SPOUSE DOESN'T WORK?

If one spouse has absolutely no earned income, a *spousal IRA* may be established as a separate IRA for the nonearning spouse. A total of up to $2,250 annually can be contributed to the two accounts combined, divided in any way desired except that neither account may receive more than $2,000. In this case, the couple must file a joint tax return. In most other respects the spousal IRA functions like a regular IRA account, and no contribution can be made for a nonearning spouse who has reached age seventy and a half, even if the earning spouse is younger.

WHEN CAN I TAKE THE MONEY OUT?

You can begin to take withdrawals (distributions) without penalty when you reach age fifty-nine and a half, and you *must* begin withdrawals before the end of the year in which you reach age seventy and a half. Between those two ages, the law gives you complete flexibility; you can withdraw any amount when you wish, at your discretion. For convenience we will often talk about taking distributions "at retirement," but note that the law sets only the above age limits for distributions, which apply regardless of when you actually retire. If you are still working between the ages of fifty-nine and a half and seventy and a half, the law permits you to make contributions, or to withdraw funds, or both. All distributions from an IRA are taxed as ordinary income in the year received. For further information on distributions, see appendix C.

CAN I HAVE MORE THAN ONE IRA ACCOUNT?

Absolutely. There's no requirement that you limit your IRA to a single sponsor. You can have as many separate IRAs as you want, as long as your *combined* contributions to all of them do not exceed $2,000 annually (or $2,250 for an IRA and a spousal IRA). For more on this subject, see chapter 5.

WHAT IF I CAN'T SAVE?

The IRA is meant to reward saving. But if you are one of those who can't save out of current income, there may still be a way to enjoy the tax benefits of an IRA. Do you have an existing savings account? Do you own stocks or bonds that you are holding as a retirement nest egg? Those existing savings are a potential tax deduction. You can take $2,000 (or less) out of an existing account, put it in an IRA, and get your tax deduction (as long as you have $2,000 of earned income that year). Of course, you will eventually pay tax on the money when you take it out, but meanwhile you enjoy the IRA double tax advantage. You save tax on the contribution *now* and the money compounds tax-free until withdrawn.

Two warnings: first, if you take the money out before age fifty-nine and a half, you will pay a penalty tax. So don't move savings dollars into an IRA unless there's at least a reasonable chance that you will leave them there for five years or more—long enough for the tax advantages to outweigh the penalty (see chapter 6). Second, if you are thinking of raising $2,000 by selling shares of a stock that you have owned for a long time, or some other long-term investment, you may have to pay a capital gains tax on the sale.

ADJUSTING YOUR TAX WITHHOLDING

Another helpful point: you don't have to wait until the following April 15 to get the benefit of the IRA tax saving. If putting dollars aside in your IRA leaves you pinched for cash—and that will probably be true for most of us—you are entitled to have your income tax withholding adjusted downward to reflect the amount of the tax saving. You can file a revised Form W-4 with your employer at any time to request a change in your withholding allowances. Your employer should have copies of Form W-4 available, and page 2 of the form provides a worksheet for figuring your allowances. Unless you prefer to have your taxes overwithheld in order to receive a refund later on, by all means take advantage of this offset.

We have now covered the basic rules on IRAs. You will find a more detailed set of rules on distributions and other matters in appendix C. But let's move on to the most important subject of all—how your IRA dollars should be invested.

I

MAKING YOUR IRA DOLLARS GROW

1

INVESTING WITH BANKS AND MONEY MARKET FUNDS

Now that you have decided to open an IRA, where should you actually put your money?

Many people will open their IRA wherever it seems most convenient. They will be content with the tax deduction and not give much thought to anything else. That will be unfortunate and shortsighted. The most critical question for the success of your IRA is where to put your IRA dollars—how you *invest* your IRA contributions.

If you are already an experienced investor, your IRA choices should give you no problem. But the average person will be confused and not know where to turn. Banks, brokerage firms, and other IRA sponsors can hardly be expected to give impartial investment advice. But with the following guidelines and information, you should be able to choose an investment approach for your IRA that will fit your own needs and make your IRA surprisingly successful.

Before we look at the investment possibilities in detail, a word of reassurance. Whatever beginning investment choice you make can easily be changed. Fortunately, the IRA rules allow you a lot of freedom to switch from one investment to another during the life of your IRA. Later on we will discuss the question of changing investments in some detail. For now, remember that you will have all the flexibility you need to make changes, if you wish, in investment vehicles.

A blizzard of IRA advertising began before January 1982, and at times it appeared that every institution was promising the investor a 12 percent return, with anywhere from $500,000 to $1,000,000 at the end of the rainbow. And if a bank promised you a return of 12 percent for thirty years or more, with your account fully guaranteed by the government, wouldn't that be good enough?

Whether 12 percent is actually an adequate rate of interest is a question we will discuss later on. But one thing is certain: no one is really promising 12 percent, or any other rate, for more than a brief period. Those thirty-year projections in the advertisements are only illustrations of what you *might* have in thirty years *if* the rates were to stay at 12 percent. Read the fine print.

What you will actually earn is much less certain. A typical bank plan will give guarantees, but only for a limited time. For example, it may guarantee that this year's contribution will earn a fixed interest rate for eighteen or thirty months. But there's no guarantee of the rate that will be offered on renewal, or of the rate that will be offered a year from now on next year's contribution. Insurance companies also are avoiding longer-term guarantees, and mutual funds and brokerage firms, by their nature, can't guarantee any fixed rate of return at all.

There is no magic way to select the best IRA investment. It's not a matter of simply shopping around for the highest guaranteed return—you will have to consider different types of investments and take a little time to understand the advantages and disadvantages of each.

A good way to begin is to list the questions that should be asked about each possible IRA investment:

1. How safe is my money? Will the value of my account fluctuate?

2. What rate will my money earn?

3. How certain are the earnings?

4. Will I keep up with inflation? What sort of long-term growth can I hope for?

5. How easily can I switch my investment?

With those questions in mind, let's look at opening an IRA with a bank or a money market fund.

BANKS AND OTHER FRIENDLY INSTITUTIONS

Let us first consider banks, a term I will use to cover not only commercial banks but also thrift institutions—savings and loans, savings banks, and credit unions. From the standpoint of your IRA, these all form one group with similar features.

There are two common opinions about banks, both of which are extreme. There are people who feel that because bank savings deposits are insured, the banks are the only safe and sensible place to invest money, and that all other investments are dangerous speculation. Since this belief approaches a religion for some people, I am a bit hesitant about commenting on it. After all, you can't blame people for wanting safety.

But life is full of risks, and sometimes people carefully avoid an obvious risk only to be tripped up by a less obvious one. Investors who kept their money in savings banks through the 1970s had their dollars insured, true enough, but they saw the *real value* of those dollars virtually *cut in half* by inflation. It was a difficult decade, but investors who worried more about inflation and less about government guarantees ended up with better results.

The other point of view about banks is just as mistaken. Remembering all the years when banks paid low interest rates to their retail depositors, some investors now refuse to consider bank accounts as a serious investment. This point of view ignores the revolution that has taken place in the savings industry. Until the mid-1970s, there was a wide difference between the "retail" rate of interest that a small saver could get at his local bank or savings and loan association and the often much higher "wholesale" or "market" rates that could be earned on investments of $10,000, $100,000, or more. The money market mutual funds were instrumental in changing that situation by making it possible for the average investor to obtain those higher "market" rates. To keep from losing all their depositors, the banks were allowed to offer new types of deposit arrangements under which they, too, now can pay market rates of interest to their ordinary depositors.

For the average investor, earning market interest rates has a double significance: you are earning as much as the large investor, and your investment is likely to keep up with the rate of inflation. With everyone having become acutely inflation conscious, large investors have become increasingly reluctant to lend money, even for short periods of time, unless they are compensated for the rate of inflation. So market rates of interest—for example, the rates the U.S. Treasury has to pay when it borrows by selling short-term Treasury bills or intermediate-term Treasury notes—are likely to be at least as high as the expected rate of inflation. And with the banks offering a whole array of certificates that reflect these market rates, a bank IRA should let you keep up with inflation, and may at times put you moderately ahead.

There's a completely different reason why some people avoid bank savings accounts: the interest earned on bank accounts is usually fully taxable. But this doesn't matter in an IRA, since the earnings accumulate tax-free. Outside of your IRA, you may have good reason to buy municipal bonds, which pay tax-exempt interest, or perhaps to invest only for long-term capital gains, on which the tax rates are reduced. But in your IRA, earnings or gains from one source are as good as another, because it's all tax-free.

A scorecard for bank IRAs might look something like this:

Pluses: You can't lose money in a bank savings account, and your account is guaranteed up to $100,000 by the Federal Deposit Insurance Corporation (FDIC) or Federal Savings and Loan Insurance Corporation (FSLIC). Your deposit doesn't change in value except as it earns interest. You know the exact rate of interest you will earn, though only for a specified period. And over the long term, your average interest rate is quite likely to exceed the rate of inflation by a modest amount, though there is certainly no guarantee. It is also worth noting that bank fees for handling your IRA are quite low (generally less than $10 per year), and many banks charge nothing at all.

Minuses: Earnings are usually limited to current short-term interest rates, for better or worse. Also, to get the best rates offered by the bank, you may have to invest your account in certificates for specific time periods. If you switch your account away from the bank before these certificates mature, you will incur the well-known "substantial penalty for early withdrawal," with a usual loss of six months' interest.

An incidental point: since an important advantage of a bank IRA is the FDIC or FSLIC guarantee of bank deposits, what happens when your IRA grows over the $100,000 guarantee limit? That's hardly a problem. It's likely that the $100,000 limit will have been raised by that time because of inflation. If not, divide your IRA among two or more banks and do not leave more than the insured limit in any one account. Incidentally, you should note that your IRA is insured for the full $100,000, no matter how many other insured accounts you have at the same bank or thrift institution.

WHO SHOULD INVEST WITH THE BANKS?

The bank IRA is, first, for the person who will only feel comfortable with a government guarantee of his or her savings. Back in the days when banks paid only 5 or 5.75 percent in interest, the financial penalty for staying with a bank was substantial. Now the banks pay well enough so that a bank IRA can be a perfectly rational choice for some people, and the results of a bank IRA should be respectable, though not brilliant.

A bank may also be appropriate if you are getting close to retirement, or if for some reason you want to withdraw your IRA money in a few years and be sure of how many dollars will be there.

If you do decide on a bank IRA, which bank and bank certificates of deposit (CDs) are best? Do some comparison shopping—compare the different certificates offered. The certificates may range in length from six months to as long as four or five years, and the variety has become bewildering, partly because the banks are no longer under any limits as to the interest rate they can pay on retirement plan certificates of eighteen months or longer. (The credit unions have this same freedom for *any* time period.) There are fixed-rate certificates, and there are certificates on which the rate is adjusted periodically in line with some market rate such as the rates on Treasury bills or notes. In December 1982, the banks started offering new accounts that were competitive with money market fund accounts, but with the minimum deposit tentatively fixed at $2,500.

The same interest rates can result in different earnings, depending on whether interest is compounded daily, quarterly, annually, or on some other schedule. For example, 12 percent interest *compounded annually* produces an *annual yield* of just 12 percent—$12 of interest for every $100 invested. But 12 percent compounded *quarterly* gives you an annual yield of 12.55 percent, and 12 percent compounded *daily* produces a yield of 12.94 percent. So compare the actual yields that the certificates produce. A bank employee should verify just how many dollars per year your certificate will yield per $1,000 invested.

The banks generally let you start your IRA with a very low minimum deposit. Each bank has its own schedule—many of the thrift institutions will let you start your account with $100 or less. Some of the commercial banks have moderately higher minimums ($250, for example), but as an alternative will let you arrange regular transfers from your checking account at a specified rate such as $10 weekly. But be careful: if you are thinking of a bank plan with low minimums, make sure that you are not being penalized by accepting the standard "passbook" rate of interest or some other low rate.

Some other warnings: be wary of bank accounts or CDs with an interest rate tied to the "discounted" U.S. Treasury bill rate, which is sometimes substantially lower than other market interest rates. Also, remember that certificates have to be renewed when they expire; in many cases, the bank will renew the same certificate again automatically at maturity unless it has specific instructions from you. The renewal may not be to your advantage.

Some people choose shorter-term or longer-term bank CDs depending on whether they think interest rates are going up or down. In theory, that's a perfectly intelligent approach, but it's not easy to apply. The most reputable economists and investment experts in the United States have failed miserably in their interest-rate predictions, and it may not be realistic to think that you (or I) will do any better. If you don't want to be in the position of making interest-rate forecasts, I suggest choosing bank certificates according to these simple rules. If you expect to keep your IRA in the bank indefinitely, and have no intention of switching investments, select the CD with the *highest effective yield*, whatever its maturity. On the other hand, if you want to stay flexible and retain some ability to switch from a bank IRA to some other IRA without a penalty, review the various CDs the bank offers and look carefully at those with the highest effective yield—say in the top 1 or $1^1/_2$ percent—and pick whichever CD in this top group has the *shortest maturity*. Use exactly the same approach at every renewal date.

What if you have bought a longer-term CD—say at 9 percent—and interest rates have risen sharply and the bank is now offering 13 percent? If the differential is wide enough, you may actually be better off paying the "substantial penalty for early withdrawal" (loss of six months' interest) in order to switch. Ask a bank employee to help you with the calculation. Incidentally, while banks must impose a penalty by law, they are *not* required to impose it on a retirement account being withdrawn by a holder who has reached age fifty-nine and a half; make sure that your bank's rules give the benefit of this exemption if you qualify. (And you can usually withdraw the accumulated *interest* on a certificate without a bank penalty at any time.)

Banks have one advantage I have avoided mentioning—they're convenient. Your bank may be the *easiest* place to have your IRA plan. You can walk in to make your deposits; you can usually start with a low minimum and make your deposits in small amounts, if you wish. The bank can also arrange for regular transfers from your checking account, and there will usually be someone available to talk to about your plan.

I haven't mentioned convenience earlier because I am hoping you won't be swayed by it. As your IRA builds, the way you manage it can make a difference of thousands of dollars every year. If a bank plan is the best for you—fine. But if it makes better sense for you to have your IRA at a brokerage firm, or at a mutual fund, then it is certainly worth the extra trouble of using the mail or making an occasional trip across town. And the same principle applies in the case of anyone who is trying to sell you an IRA—don't let convenience distract you from the main objective of building your money up over the long term in the best way.

MONEY MARKET FUNDS

Almost everyone has become familiar with money market funds in recent years. The money market fund is a type of mutual fund, but of a very special sort.

Money market funds began their spectacular rise in the mid-1970s. Interest rates were rising, as reflected in such "wholesale" items as U.S. Treasury bills and large bank certificates of deposit. But small bank depositors, as we noted above, were still only earning 5 percent or thereabouts on their money, under antiquated rules that had not been revised. The happy solution invented by the mutual fund industry was a new type of mutual fund that accepted relatively low amounts from investors and, with this pooled money, bought Treasury bills, bank CDs, and other short-term debt instruments common in the "wholesale" market and yielding a market rate of return.

The money market funds had become a $200 billion industry by 1982, and banks of all types were painfully aware that many of those billions had been transferred out of their vaults. The leading money funds have held their operating expenses, including management fees, to less than 1 percent of assets; they have been able to pass on to shareholders all but a small part of the yield on their bank CDs and other investments. Yields are compounded daily.

The money funds have also attracted shareholders by special services—most notably, the ability to write checks on a shareholder's account (usually in minimum amounts of $500), with the depositor continuing to earn interest on the money until the check clears. And most of them handle their accounting so that the only variation is in the interest rate, or yield—the value of your principal stays the same, just as in a bank account; you can always take out just as much as you put in, plus whatever interest you have earned. Needless to say, virtually all money market funds offer ready-made IRA plans that make it simple to start your IRA.

How safe are the money funds? Banks are quick to point out that money market fund accounts, unlike bank savings accounts, carry no federal guarantee.

The safety of the money market funds rests on the safety of the investments making up their portfolios—generally U.S. Treasury bills, other short-term government obligations, large bank CDs, and short-term obligations of corporations, termed "commercial paper." These latter items are, in effect, simply "IOUs" of banks and corporations. In the case of the better-quality banks and corporations, these IOUs are generally regarded as safe investments, and the historical record fully confirms this view.

Nevertheless, from time to time, doomsday-type articles appear, warning of serious risks in the money funds. The pessimists claim that the corporate IOUs held by many funds, and even the bank IOUs, could become worthless in a massive national financial crisis. No one can be absolutely sure that this is impossible. The last time we had a crisis approaching that scale was in the 1930s. Could it happen again? The United States has managed to avoid a serious financial disaster for almost fifty years, and it is hard to believe that the government and the Federal Reserve, with the massive powers they now possess, would ever again stand by and let a downward spiral re-create the Great Depression. While there is no way of completely ruling out that possibility, I wouldn't let this hypothetical risk scare me out of the money market funds—or out of corporate bonds or common stocks, either.

But while I am not seriously worried about a 1930s-type crisis, it is always possible that one or two of the banks or corporations to which a money fund has lent short-term funds might unexpectedly default. The money funds are generally careful to lend only to companies with high credit ratings, and they have had no reported problems of default in recent years. But what if a portfolio item should go sour? Consider a billion-dollar money fund, which might be lending its cash to fifty different banks and corporations, with an average of $20 million to each. The complete loss of one of these investments would have the effect of slicing 2 percent off the fund's yield for the year—a loss, but not a disaster.

Or imagine a worse case, where a fund lends 5 percent of its assets (ordinarily 5 percent is the maximum that legally can be lent to a single borrower) to a bank or corporation, and then faces a default. Assuming a total loss of the investment (a partial recovery is more likely), your yield for the year would be cut by 5 percent— say from an expected 12 percent to 7 percent, or from 10 percent to 5 percent. Your principal would still be intact. The results would not be what you hoped for, but still far short of a catastrophe. The risk is there, but it is certainly manageable.

I have been surprised to learn that there is another risk, in this case quite imaginary, which some people attach to money funds. This worry concerns the fund's manager and the manager's solvency, especially in the case of funds managed by brokerage firms. What happens to Merrill Lynch's money funds, the question goes, if Merrill Lynch runs into financial difficulties? Or Dean Witter Reynolds's Intercapital Liquid Asset Fund, or Bache's MoneyMart Assets?

11

Table 1
SELECTED LARGER MONEY MARKET FUNDS
(that offer IRA plans to the general investor)

Name and Address	Assets (millions) 6/30/82	Affiliation
*Alliance Capital Reserves, Inc. 140 Broadway New York, NY 10005 (800) 221-5672	$ 1,505	B
†Capital Preservation Fund, Inc. 755 Page Mill Rd. Palo Alto, CA 94304 (800) 227-8380	1,966	I
*Current Interest, Inc. 333 Clay St., Suite 4300 Houston, TX 77002 (713) 751-2400 (collect)	1,552	GL
Daily Cash Accumulation Fund, Inc. 3600 S. Yosemite St. Denver, CO 80237 (800) 525-9310	5,432	GL
*Delaware Cash Reserve, Inc. 7 Penn Center Plaza Philadelphia, PA 19103 (800) 523-1918	2,287	GL
Dreyfus Liquid Assets 767 Fifth Ave. New York, NY 10153 (800) 223-5525	10,039	GN
*Fidelity Cash Reserves 82 Devonshire St. Boston, MA 02109 (800) 225-6190	3,866	GN
Fidelity Daily Income Trust (See Fidelity Cash Reserves)	3,711	GN
†First Variable Rate Fund for Government Income, Inc. 1700 Pennsylvania Ave. NW Washington, DC 20006 (800) 368-2748	1,402	I
†Fund for Government Investors, Inc. 1735 K St. NW	1,312	I

Washington, DC 20006
(202) 861-1800 (collect)

InterCapital Liquid Asset Fund (Dean Witter) 5 World Trade Center New York, NY 10048 (800) 221-2685	9,432	B
*Kemper Money Market Fund, Inc. 120 South LaSalle St. Chicago, IL 60603 (800) 621-1048	3,547	GL
Merrill Lynch Ready Assets Trust One Liberty Plaza New York, NY 10080 (212) 637-6310	22,217	B
*MoneyMart Assets, Inc. 100 Gold St. New York, NY 10292 (212) 791-7123	3,977	B
*National Liquid Reserves, Inc. 605 Third Ave. New York, NY 10158 (800) 223-7757	1,944	GL
*†NRTA-AARP U.S. Government Money Market Trust 421 Seventh Ave. Pittsburgh, PA 15219 (800) 245-4770	4,436	I
Oppenheimer Money Market Fund, Inc. 2 Broadway New York, NY 10004 (212) 668-5100	1,639	GL
*Reserve Fund, Inc. 810 Seventh Ave. New York, NY 10019 (800) 223-5547	2,928	I
*T. Rowe Price Prime Reserve Fund, Inc. 100 East Pratt St. Baltimore, MD 21202 (800) 638-5660	3,437	GN

Affiliations: B—Broker affiliated; GL—Affiliated with mutual fund group (load—see chapter 2); GN—Affiliated with mutual fund group (no-load—see chapter 2); I—Independent.
  *Starting minimum of $1,000 or less for IRAs.
  †Invests only in U.S. government and agency obligations.

The question is actually a perfectly reasonable one. But even complete bankruptcy on the part of the sponsor (and I am not suggesting that any such event is likely) should not affect the financial strength of a fund. There are very careful laws to protect mutual funds from the sins of their sponsors. Money market funds, like all mutual funds, are tightly regulated by the Securities and Exchange Commission (SEC) under the Investment Company Act of 1940, with strict rules for shareholder protection. The actual assets of a money fund, or any other type of mutual fund, are generally in the hands of a bank custodian, not the sponsor. The funds are also required to carry fidelity bond insurance against theft, fraud, and similar risks. Of course, bankruptcy of a sponsor would probably mean poor customer service for a while, but under normal procedures, you could go directly to the custodian bank, get your money out, and put it in another money fund with smarter managers.

What will a money fund do for your IRA? The results with a money fund will not differ greatly from those with a bank. Both pay yields that are tied roughly to prevailing short-term market interest rates. Much of the time in recent years the money funds have yielded more than bank CDs, but at times the advantage has been reversed. You will earn the going short-term market interest rate from your money fund, less a fraction to cover the fund's expenses. As we pointed out earlier, that should usually be sufficient to keep you modestly ahead of inflation. Your principal will hold steady and will be safeguarded.

But there are differences between a money fund IRA and a bank IRA. In the first place, as we have discussed, while your principal is probably safe in the money fund, it is *not* government-guaranteed. And your yield is never fixed, as in a bank certificate, but varies from day to day with the fund's investments. Many newspapers carry weekly listings of current money fund yields, and the fund will usually give you the current yield by phone. You will have to wait for your statements (monthly or quarterly) from the fund to know exactly what you have earned.

One convenience of the money funds, the check-writing privilege, is of no use in an IRA. But the fact that you can take your money out at any time without penalty is a clear advantage for anyone who plans to switch his or her IRA among different investments. If you pick a money fund that is part of a "family of funds," you can have the convenience of simple switching from your money fund to other types of funds, such as common stock funds and bond funds—the specifics depending on the fund group you join. On the other hand, if you leave your dollars at the money fund, there is nothing to do, compared with a bank; there are no certificates to renew and your money just keeps earning interest.

Some money funds have very low starting minimums. Most have starting minimums ranging from $1,000 to $5,000, but these are often reduced or waived completely for IRAs. The fund's servicing bank will usually impose fees for acting as custodian of your IRA; the annual maintenance fee should be under $10.

Who should have a money market fund IRA? In large part, the same kind of person for whom bank IRAs are suitable. The money funds provide a high degree of safety like the banks, and the value of your investment will not fluctuate. If you expect to take your IRA money out within a few years after you contribute, then a money fund, like a bank, makes excellent sense. And if you want this type of investment now, but want to be free later to switch part or all of your money at your discretion into another type of investment, the money fund will give you complete flexibility in a way that bank CDs cannot.

The bank IRAs and the money fund IRAs are the simplest, most conservative types of investment. That's not necessarily bad—you won't make a killing with either of these, but neither will you make any serious mistakes. With the changes that have occurred in the savings industry, the value of your account is not likely to fall seriously behind the rate of inflation and will more probably stay a little ahead of it. If you prefer to accept a moderate return and keep your risks to a minimum, either of these approaches makes perfectly good sense.

If you have decided to invest in a money fund IRA, which one should you pick? Many newspapers carry weekly listings of money fund yields, and they are filled with money fund advertisements. Unless you are absolutely convinced that you will never want to switch into another type of mutual fund, you can gain convenience by picking a money fund that is part of a fund group, or "family of funds." Since the differences among money funds generally are minor, you should pick the fund group that attracts you most for other reasons (see chapter 2).

If the "fund group" approach doesn't interest you, the two

criteria to consider in a money fund are convenience and safety. The most convenient fund is one where either the fund office or its custodian bank is located near enough to you so that you can make your deposits in person, without being subject to the delays of the mails. If that isn't practical, you might pick a fund whose custodian bank is close enough so that your checks to the bank, and its confirmations back to you, have a chance of arriving promptly. But don't let this become a major point; you can use a money fund three thousand miles away, and the inconvenience will only be minor.

Safety is a matter for your own judgment and preference. As we have shown, most money funds involve very small risks compared with other types of investments. But there are variations among funds. Some money funds opt for complete safety by investing only in U.S. government obligations; others extend their investments to the highest-grade bank certificates of deposit and corporate commercial paper; still others will lend to a wider range of banks and corporations in order to earn a somewhat higher yield. Generally speaking, the more risk, the more yield; but the maximum yield differentials are often no more than 1 to 1.5 percent, reflecting the fact that even the higher-yield funds are taking only very minor risks by most standards.

The basic investment policy of each fund is stated in its prospectus, which usually can be obtained with a phone call. An excellent compact guide to the money funds is Donoghue's *Money Fund Directory*, available at $15 and revised twice annually (Box 540, Holliston, MA 01746, [617] 429-5930). It is published by the same organization that issues the expensive weekly Donoghue's *Money Fund Report*, the standard statistical service on the money funds. Lists of money funds are available from the Investment Company Institute, the trade association of the mutual fund industry (see chapter 2). There are far too many money funds to describe them all here, but table 1 lists the addresses of a few of the largest and indicates which ones invest in U.S. government securities only.

A money fund may or may not be suitable for your IRA. But all investors owe the money funds a vote of thanks for having broken the old, outmoded savings patterns and for giving the average investor flexibility, convenience, and a fair return on his money.

2

INVESTING IN COMMON STOCKS AND COMMON STOCK FUNDS

So far we have been talking about the simplest and most conservative investments—those that do not fluctuate in value but that build up your dollars by compounding interest payments, with your money committed only for relatively short periods.

Now I want to leap toward the other end of the spectrum to look at a completely different type of investment—common stocks. Common stocks are an important long-range investment about which most people know much too little. Of course, some readers of this book are thoroughly familiar with common stocks. But many others undoubtedly have been frightened—wrongly, I think—into believing that common stocks are too dangerous or too complicated for the average person's savings.

Common stocks are no great mystery and, rightly managed, they can be useful to even the smallest investor. They have proved more profitable than many other types of investments, and they deserve serious consideration by everyone who expects to leave money in an IRA over the long term—say for five years or more.

Common stocks represent the ownership of corporations. Each share of stock is, literally, a share of ownership in a business. If the business is profitable and grows successfully, the value of each share will grow over time, and the portion of profits that can be paid out to the shareholders as dividends will grow as well.

Let's look at the record. The longest available study of common stock investments shows that from 1926 to 1981, a period of fifty-six years, money invested in U.S. common stocks grew at an average compounded rate of 9.1 percent a year (Roger G. Ibbotson and Rex A. Sinquefield, *Stocks, Bonds, Bills, and Inflation: The Past and the Future*, The Financial Analysts Research Foundation, 1982. The common stock performance figures are based on the Standard & Poor's 500 Stock Index, adjusted to include reinvestment of dividends). In this age of high returns, 9.1 percent may not sound very exciting, but in the same period the rate of inflation averaged only 3 percent a year. The common stock investor averaged over 6 percent a year *better* than inflation.

Since statistics dating back to the 1920s and 1930s might not be meaningful today, let's concentrate on the period after World War II. From 1947 to 1981, inflation averaged 4.3 percent annually, but money invested in common stocks grew at an average annual rate of *10.8 percent*. The net advantage to the common stock investor was still *better than 6 percent* a year. By way of comparison, money invested in U.S. Treasury bills over this postwar period would have grown at only 4.2 percent annually—slightly less than the inflation rate—and money in the average savings account would have done no better.

These figures are, in a nutshell, the reason why common stocks are worth considering for your IRA. I have a special reason for wanting to set this alternative in front of you right now. Bank advertising on IRAs has been so pervasive that some people apparently think that an IRA *must* be invested with a bank or savings and loan institution. This is simply not true. You do have a choice, and common stocks should be seriously considered.

The performance figures I have quoted describe the *average* return that common stocks have earned for their owners over long periods. But when you invest in common stocks, your results may be very different from the average.

This is worth a word of explanation. If you are investing in money market funds, for example, the differences in rate of return among the various different funds at any given time is not likely to be great, and whatever the average rate is, your own rate will not be far from it. The same is true of the banks, which also are tied quite closely to the prevailing market rates of interest. But there is no such uniformity with common stocks. There are thousands of corporations in the United States, and the rates at which they earn and grow vary tremendously. Prices of common stocks, besides reflecting these real differences, are subjected to broad price swings because of people's expectations and their confidence (or lack of it) in the individual company or in the stock market as a whole.

So if you invest in common stocks, the results will vary greatly depending on your skill in selection and timing. Over the fifty-six- and thirty-five-year periods quoted above, if your common stock investments had been managed by a superior manager, the results would have been substantially better than the averages. With inferior management, of course, you might have done substantially worse.

Are common stocks still a viable investment today? I believe they are. True, the economy is growing more sluggishly than in the early postwar years, and businesses face many problems that hardly existed twenty or thirty years ago. But there are also new opportunities—one need only look at the rapid growth in computers, cable television, health services, convenience foods, and financial services, to name a few sectors. The U.S. economy will continue to change and grow; many industries will expand, and some companies will continue to be successful and to generate substantial rewards for their owners. Careful investment in common stocks will continue to be one of the best ways of making your money grow over the years.

There's another reason for considering common stocks for your long-term investment program. That reason is inflation. While economic growth may be less than it was twenty years ago, the rate of inflation, which we touched on earlier, has soared. Even if there is some success in controlling inflation, most economists predict that the inflation rate will stay substantially above the 2 to 3 percent range that the country enjoyed in the 1950s and 1960s.

What does this mean for common stocks? Remember that stocks represent the ownership of corporate assets. Depending on the type of company, these assets may include real estate, factories, oil reserves, mines, forests—much of the accumulated wealth of the country. Historically, the dollar value of these assets rises along with inflation, and the companies rise in value as well.

The market prices of common stocks often seem out of step with inflation, forging ahead in some years and lagging behind in others. But over the long run, as we saw earlier, common stocks have not only kept their owners even with inflation but have far outperformed the inflation rate.

If common stocks are such good investments, why do so many people avoid them? One reason, certainly, is that common stock prices do fluctuate—sometimes violently. Look at figure 1. There is no mistaking the long-term uptrend, but the common stock investor had to ride out severe declines in 1957, 1962, and later years. Some people find these fluctuations simply too disturbing to live with, even if they recognize the long-term growth trend. If peace of mind is more important to you than maximum return, you certainly have a right to your preference.

There is another reason why common stocks are out of favor with many people in the 1980s. Its origin lies in the history of the 1970s. Common stocks had a prolonged boom in the postwar period until 1968, with a final spurt in 1971–72. Stock prices, as measured by the popular averages, tripled and quadrupled. Declines during this period generally ended quickly. As the enthusiasm grew, so did speculation, and prices of highly touted "growth stocks" such as Xerox, Avon, Polaroid, and others rose to astronomical heights relative to current earnings.

Then the boom collapsed and prices began a long, painful readjustment downward. The readjustment was made many times worse by the Arab oil embargo in 1973, the resulting explosion in oil prices, and the crippling of economic growth. By late 1974, the stock market averages were down almost 50 percent from their 1972 peaks, in the worst decline of the postwar period.

The recovery after this decline was uneven. Despite many successes in individual stocks and industries, the stock market as a whole spent most of the 1970s in a hangover from the previous boom. While prices of gold, real estate, and many other assets were soaring, common stocks stayed in the doldrums.

Figure 1
STOCK PRICES AND PRICE-EARNINGS RATIOS

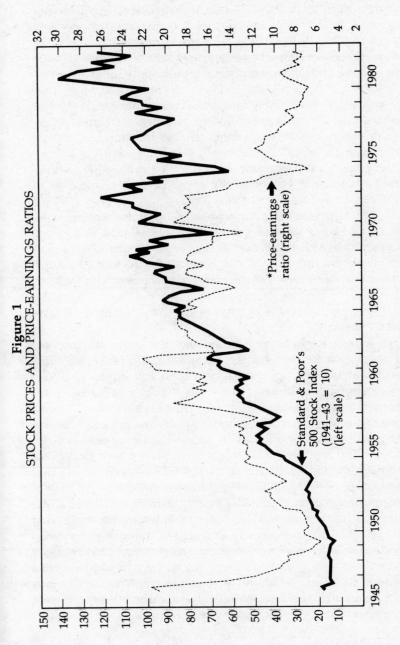

*The price-earnings ratio is calculated by dividing the price index at the end of each calendar quarter by earnings for the previous twelve months.

21

As a result, a whole generation of people under age thirty has learned to think of common stocks in negative terms. I believe history will show this pessimism is mistaken, as was the overoptimism of the late 1960s. Taking a longer-term point of view, the result of the 1970s may well have been to create historic bargains in common stock prices, and promising opportunities for investors in the 1980s.

The most common standard by which professionals judge whether stocks are cheap or expensive is the relation of stock prices to company earnings. When the *price-earnings ratio* (or *price-earnings multiple*) is high, stocks are relatively expensive; when it is low, they are relatively cheap. Another measure is the dividend *yield* an investor can obtain by buying stocks. In this case, when the yield is low, stocks are expensive, and vice versa.

In 1972, when the long market boom was in its last stage, the average common stock was selling at about eighteen times that year's earnings, and the average dividend yield to investors was a meager 3 percent. In early 1982, by contrast, the average stock was selling at less than eight times earnings and the average dividend yield was over 6 percent. Relative to earnings and dividends, stock prices were more than 50 percent below the level of ten years earlier.

The broken line in figure 1 clearly shows the dramatic drop in price-earnings ratios over the last decade. During early 1982, not only could an investor be sure that he was not buying stocks at the top of a boom, he could reasonably hope that he was buying near the bottom of a long price swing.

At this point, let me summarize what you can and cannot expect from common stocks. You'll notice that I have been talking in terms of probabilities. Nothing is guaranteed where stocks are concerned—there's no assurance of the rate of return, and the current value of your stocks will fluctuate with the market. At times, particularly in the first few years, the market value of your investment may be less than the amount you put in. An intelligent selection of stocks is absolutely essential—a poor selection will bring disaster. But with good selection, and patience, I believe that over the long term your investment will grow at a rate that will more than repay you for all the fluctuations and risks.

Two warnings: first, we are talking about the long run. It isn't wise to put your IRA dollars (or any other money) in common stocks if you expect to draw it out in two or three years. A one-year or two-year dip in stock prices is possible at any time, and one of these dips may come at the wrong time for you. If you will need your money quickly, pick an investment that doesn't fluctuate.

Second, I pointed out that common stock investments require patience. It isn't just patience; it takes a little fortitude. Many investors succumb to panic when stock prices are dropping. No one knows when the drop will end, and people forget that their stocks (if well chosen) represent ownership shares in prime companies. Investors begin to think of their stocks as only pieces of paper and so, at just the wrong time, just when prices are at their lowest, many amateurs (and many professionals) sell out.

In difficult times, remember there is nothing foolish or wildly speculative about keeping part or all of your money invested in major U.S. corporations. With a little fortitude—or perhaps simply with an ability to ignore the newspaper headlines—you may find yourself a successful common stock investor, with surprisingly good results.

HOW TO BUY STOCKS

Let's assume that you have decided to invest your IRA dollars in common stocks. How do you go about it? When buying stocks, be sure that: (1) the stocks are carefully selected and bought at prices that represent good value; (2) they are then just as carefully *managed*, which means above all being prompt in selling a stock when it no longer represents good value, and replacing it with something better; and (3) you have *diversified* your holdings over enough issues so that you are not tied too heavily to any one company or industry.

If you know enough about common stocks to choose and manage them yourself, or if you know a broker in whom you have confidence, you can open your IRA with a brokerage firm (see chapter 4).

Another way of buying common stocks, and one that is probably practical for a larger number of investors, is through common stock mutual funds. For those who are not familiar with common stock funds, here is a word of introduction.

The most familiar type of mutual fund today is the money market fund. But before the meteoric rise of the money funds, the dominant mutual funds were common stock funds, and many people thought of mutual funds mainly in terms of common stocks.

A mutual fund—whatever the type of investment—is basically a way of pooling the money of many investors, large and small, so that their investments can be managed effectively and cheaply as a single unit. A mutual fund is technically an open-end investment company—"open-end" because the fund stands ready to sell (issue) additional shares to investors who want to put money in the pool, or to buy back (redeem) shares from investors who want to take their money out. (In chapter 4, I will have a word to say about "closed-end" funds, which operate with a fixed number of shares.)

Note that you are buying *shares* in the pool. In a common stock fund, the value of a share depends on the market value of the stocks the fund owns. If those stocks (the "portfolio securities") go up in price, the price of your fund shares will go up also, and vice versa. This is in contrast to a money fund, where the price is usually held constant at $1 per share. Prices of most funds are calculated daily and are listed in the financial sections of major newspapers.

A mutual fund has certain advantages. First and foremost, no matter how small your starting investment, you immediately get professional management of your money. Second, the funds are diversified. The average common stock fund may own anywhere from twenty-five to two hundred different stocks. This is enough to spread the risk, so that if any single investment goes sour, it won't be a disaster for the fund's total results. Until your IRA gets very large, this kind of diversification will be impractical if you buy individual stocks directly.

Third, the funds are convenient. Most mutual funds offer ready-made IRA plans that make it simple to start your IRA. Generally the same bank that handles the fund's banking requirements also acts as custodian of your IRA plan.

If you have money in one or more funds, you can still easily keep track of your investments, watch the fund's performance, and generally be aware of how your IRA is doing. You can buy additional shares with a check to the fund or to the custodian bank; if your fund is part of a larger fund group or "family of funds," you can usually arrange to make switches among funds by telephone (usually for a small fee of $5 or so).

Starting minimums for mutual funds usually range between $250 and $500, but some funds will accept less. As for fees, the funds' custodian banks generally charge between $5 and $10 annually to maintain an IRA. Some also charge a fee (typically $5) to open the account; some don't. Unless your IRA contributions are very small, the fees for mutual fund IRAs are relatively low enough so that they should not be an important consideration in your choice of fund or fund group. Note that most of the major fund groups listed in table 5 have toll-free phone numbers, making it simple to obtain this type of information and to request the fund's literature.

The limitations of a mutual fund investment are fairly obvious. If you want to control your own common stock investments in detail, a mutual fund is not for you. If you are convinced that you can get rich by putting all your money in the latest computer or medical electronic stock, you need a brokerage IRA. Common stock selection is usually best left to professionals, but some amateurs certainly have proved they can successfully manage stock investments. Some people enjoy selecting stocks so much that they will not give it up. And still others want the pleasure or reassurance of being able to talk to a broker about their investments.

CHOOSING MUTUAL FUNDS

How do you go about picking a mutual fund? As of January 1982, there were about 350 common stock funds in the United States— plus about 160 money market funds and roughly 150 funds investing in bonds or combinations of stocks and bonds.

Don't let anyone tell you that the choice among these funds is unimportant. You may have heard that professional managers, *on the average*, have not done any better in the stock market than anyone else. Some academic experts, forgetting that averages are only averages, have gone so far as to conclude that throwing darts at a stock list works as well as trusting to a professional manager. Don't believe it! Admittedly, the *average* performance of all professional managers has been mediocre. But some have been *consistently* better than average, and others have been *consistently* worse. A small number have achieved remarkable long-run records. Your job is to select one (or a few) of those that have been consistently superior.

Common stock funds are usually classified according to the degree of risk they take in pursuing growth of capital. You will find fund classifications that range from "aggressive growth" or "maximum capital gain" on through "growth" to "growth-income" and finally to "income." (See table 2 for a clarification of these terms.) The income funds are considered the most conservative, since they tend to invest in large companies like AT&T or Exxon, which pay high dividends, and where less volatility is likely both in the company's earnings and in the price of the stock.

You can expect the aggressive growth funds to show the greatest growth in value in a favorable stock market, and the greatest declines in a bad market. Conversely, a good income or growth-income fund is likely to go down relatively less in a market decline. But the quality of the management is still paramount. There are "income" funds that have consistently outperformed most of the growth funds over the years, and there are "growth" funds that have lost remarkable amounts of money for their shareholders, even in good markets.

So we return to the question of picking a superior fund management. First of all, don't look for the fund that showed the best performance in the latest year. No single year tells enough about management competence. In order to get to the head of the pack, the leading fund managers (very possibly) went to some kind of extreme position in their portfolio policy and took more risks than you want to assume. But if a fund has done consistently well over ten years—or better still, twenty years—compared with other funds and with the market averages, then the management knows what it is doing.

The most complete survey of fund performance available is probably the *Mutual Fund Performance Analysis,* published primarily for professionals by Lipper Analytical Services, Inc. (available through Lipper Analytical Distributors, Inc., 74 Trinity Pl., New York, NY 10006). This weekly service tracks the performance of over 500 funds, including about 350 common stock funds, with special quarterly issues that review performance over longer periods going back ten or twenty years. The cost of the service is prohibitive for most individuals, but you may be able to consult it at a brokerage house, library, or mutual fund office (see table 3).

A somewhat less detailed but extremely useful source is the *Wiesenberger Investment Companies Service.* The Wiesenberger annual *Investment Companies* manual is in some respects the industry

Table 2
HOW FUNDS ARE CLASSIFIED

Terms Frequently Used	Description
Common stock funds:	
Maximum capital gains Capital appreciation Aggressive growth	Funds that take substantial risks in pursuit of maximum capital appreciation, often with short-term trading and "technical" approaches aimed at anticipating market movements. Likely to invest in smaller companies. Price volatility generally high; very sharp declines possible in adverse markets.
Growth Long-term growth	Emphasis on stocks with long-term growth prospects; usually more stress on basic research and less on "technical" market analysis than in "maximum capital gains" group. Risk level and price volatility usually somewhat less.
Growth and income Growth and current income	Stocks may be chosen for growth only, or for growth and income; usually more emphasis on stocks of larger companies. More relative price stability; price volatility usually comparable to broad market averages.
Equity income Income—common stock policy	Stress on income, with growth secondary; investments likely to be in larger, well-established companies with less price volatility.
Funds owning stocks and bonds:	
Income Income—flexible policy	"Income" funds, unless otherwise specified, are likely to invest in combinations of bonds, common stocks, and (often) preferred stocks for high income, relative price stability, and (perhaps) some long-term growth.
Balanced	Balanced funds stress a combination of bonds and stocks as protection for the investor against different types of economic conditions; common stocks may be chosen for growth as well as for income.
Bond funds:	
Bond Fixed income Income—senior securities	Objective is income. Traditionally supposed to provide high relative price stability, an objective not realized recently.

Table 3
LIPPER'S TOP TWENTY-FIVE FUNDS FOR THE YEARS 1962–1981

Name	% Gain 12/31/61– 12/31/81	Annual Return (%)	Type	Assets (millions) 6/30/82
1. Templeton Growth Fund	1,677	15.5	Load	$508.2
2. International Investors	1,341	14.3	Load	203.3
3. Over-The-Counter Securities Fund	1,055	13.0	Load	45.3
4. Twentieth Century Growth Investors	1,046	13.0	No-load	261.9
5. American General Enterprise Fund	848	11.9	Load	445.9
6. Twentieth Century Select Investors	819	11.7	No-load	49.4
7. Mutual Shares Corp.	815	11.7	No-load	130.0
8. PLITREND Fund	758	11.3	No-load	16.9
9. Pioneer Fund	684	10.8	Load	887.8
10. Financial Industrial Income Fund	667	10.7	No-load	148.3
11. Value Line Fund	664	10.7	No-load	72.9
12. T. Rowe Price New Horizons Fund	608	10.3	No-load	787.6
13. Decatur Income Fund	603	10.2	Load	349.4
14. American General Harbor Fund	569	10.0	Load	109.6
15. Value Line Income Fund	567	10.0	No-load	70.5
16. Axe-Houghton Stock Fund	554	9.8	Load	105.7
17. Istel Fund	550	9.8	No-load	94.8
18. Guardian Mutual Fund	549	9.8	No-load	166.6
19. Investors Research Fund	549	9.8	Load	16.5
20. Security Investment Fund	548	9.8	Load	96.7
21. American National Growth Fund	533	9.7	Load	52.3
22. Windsor Fund	532	9.7	No-load	918.4
23. National Total Return Fund (formerly National Dividend Fund)	527	9.6	Load	81.4
24. American Mutual Fund	510	9.5	Load	478.4
25. Fidelity Puritan Fund	495	9.3	No-load	593.4

Adapted from Lipper, *Mutual Fund Performance Analysis, 12/31/81.* Figures on percentage gain assume reinvestment of all capital gains distributions and income dividends. Annual return (calculated by the author from the Lipper percentage gain figures) is the equivalent compound average annual growth rate over the whole period. No deduction has been made for the commission that would have been paid on the purchase of load fund shares. The past record should not be regarded as a prediction of future performance.

bible, with descriptions and records of all major and many secondary funds (including closed-end funds), plus a host of general articles that may be of interest if you are learning to be a mutual fund investor. There are quarterly performance updates, each showing performance ratings over a ten-year period and for shorter periods as well. (Subscription $130 annually from Warren, Gorham & Lamont, Inc., 210 South St., Boston, MA 02111, [617] 423-2020.)

A more limited but easily available quarterly performance survey is published by *Barron's*, a national financial weekly that was one of the first periodicals to track mutual fund performance regularly many years ago. The mutual fund issues appear in early February, May, August, and November. *Barron's* is carried by many libraries; it sells on newsstands for $1.25, and an annual subscription is $55 (*Barron's*, 200 Burnett Rd., Chicopee, MA 01021).

Services such as Lipper and Wiesenberger present statistics without making recommendations, and some amateurs may find themselves lost. Fortunately, recommendations are available. One excellent publication is the *United Mutual Fund Selector*, a semi-monthly newsletter on mutual funds that features a "supervised list" of about thirty common stock funds in various categories (212 Newbury St., Boston, MA 02116, annual subscription $65). If a fund is on the supervised list, you can generally be assured of its quality. The service will tell you when it thinks a fund no longer deserves to be held, and it also provides plenty of statistics and articles that will help you learn more about your investments.

Another publication that provides both knowledgeable advice and specific recommendations is *Growth Fund Guide* (Yreka, CA 96097, annual subscription $76). This monthly service emphasizes the more aggressive no-load growth funds, but lists a few middle-of-the-road funds as well. Another source is *Forbes* magazine, which every year (usually in mid-August) publishes a survey on the mutual fund industry, featuring an "honor roll" of a relatively small number of funds with outstanding records, as well as several pages of statistics covering most major funds (see table 4). If you want recommendations with a minimum of cost and reading time, *Forbes* may be the source for you (on newsstands biweekly at $2.50; annual subscription $33 from *Forbes*, 60 Fifth Ave., New York, NY 10011).

Most of these sources now provide performance statistics, which assume that all income dividends and capital gain distributions are reinvested. This is all to the good, especially for an IRA in-

Table 4
THE *FORBES* "HONOR ROLL" OF COMMON STOCK
MUTUAL FUNDS (1982)

Name	Type	Market Ratings UP	Market Ratings DOWN	Annual Return (%)	Assets (millions) (6/30/82)
AMCAP	Load	A	B	14.3	$394.0
American General Comstock	Load	B	A	15.4	153.4
American General Pace	Load	A +	A	17.0	129.7
Charter	Load	A +	B	18.0	44.7
Fidelity Magellan	Load	A +	B	19.0	146.8
International Investors	Load	A	A	19.0	203.3
Janus	No-load	A	A	18.4	44.9
Mutual Shares	No-load	B	B	18.6	130.0
Nicholas	No-load	A	B	15.4	56.1
Pioneer II	Load	B	A	18.5	485.1
Putnam-Voyager	Load	A	C	14.7	87.9
St. Paul Growth	Load	A	B	15.0	36.7
Sigma Venture Shares	Load	A +	C	14.0	22.7
Templeton Growth	Load	B	B	17.3	508.2
Twentieth Century Growth	No-load	A +	C	21.5	261.9
Twentieth Century Select	No-load	A +	B	17.9	49.4
Vance, Sanders Special	Load	A	C	15.2	86.4

Adapted from *Forbes*, August 30, 1982. The *Forbes* 1982 ratings were based on a survey of fund performance from May 26, 1970 (the bottom of the 1970 market decline), to June 30, 1982. The market ratings are based on relative performance in three "up markets" and three "down markets" during that period. The annual return is the compound average annual rate at which an investment in the fund would have grown over the whole period (without adjustment for inflation), assuming that all capital gains distributions and income dividends were reinvested, and without any deduction for the commission that would have been paid on the purchase of load fund shares. The past record should not be regarded as a prediction of future performance.

vestor. Many years ago it was more common to see performance calculated *without* the income dividends, which were shown separately as "yield." For people who live by spending their dividend income, the old distinction may be useful. But in your IRA, or in any other tax-free retirement plan, it's only the total dollar buildup that matters; the dividend yield has no separate importance. The "total return" statistics shown by these services are what you need.

The subject of taxation may need some additional explanation.

A fund can make money for its shareholders in three ways. It can own and hold stocks that rise in price, so the fund shares rise in price also; it can *sell* stocks that have risen in price and pay out the profits as capital gain distributions; or it can earn ordinary income (dividends and interest) that it pays out as income dividends, which constitute the "yield." For a taxable investor, each of these three steps has different tax consequences. But in your IRA, there are no taxes to pay until withdrawal. All dividends and capital gain distributions are plowed back into the account, and one source of additional dollars is as good as another.

A few comments about using the performance statistics: first, make sure you understand how the percentages work. Table 3, for example, tells you that Templeton Growth Fund led the pack over twenty years with a total percentage gain of 1,677 percent. That means that $1,000 invested in Templeton in December 1961 would have grown by $16,770 (1,677 percent times $1,000) to reach a final value of $17,770 (*not* $16,770). A 500 percent gain would have raised the value from $1,000 to $6,000; a 100 percent gain, from $1,000 to $2,000; and so forth.

(You'll notice that some performance statistics include an extra column showing dividend yield. If the performance figures are on a total return basis, yield has already been included—don't add it in again. The yield figure, as noted above, is useful primarily to investors who take their dividends in cash as spendable income. But it may also tell you something about a fund's policies—a high yield usually reflects investments in larger corporations and a relatively conservative investment approach.)

When you look at statistics comparing a fund's record with the market averages (such as the Dow Jones Industrial Average, the Standard & Poor's 500 Stock Index, or the New York Stock Exchange Composite Index), be careful. The market averages do *not* include income dividends, unless the statistical service makes a special adjustment. It's easy for a fund to look better than the Dow Jones Industrials if the fund's performance is credited with 2 to 8 percent a year in income dividends and the Dow Jones is not. The footnotes to the tables should tell you whether or not the averages have been adjusted to include income.

When selecting a fund, past performance may be the most important fact to look for, but it is not the only one. Be sure you understand the fund's basic investment policy and the rules under which it operates. You may find these described in the Wiesenberger handbook or occasionally in the *United Mutual Fund Selector,* but the basic source is a fund's own prospectus and its reports to shareholders.

Legally, you can't buy shares in a fund without receiving a copy of the fund's prospectus. Some prospectuses are more informative than others; in any case, see what the prospectus says about investment policies and objectives before you buy. Read the fund's recent annual and quarterly reports to shareholders in order to get a clearer idea of just what the fund is doing and what it's trying to do.

A basic difference among funds is that some funds are sold with a commission—these are known as load funds—and some are sold without a commission—these are called no-load funds. The commission charged by the load funds is generally 6 to 8.5 percent on purchases under $10,000, which means that out of your $2,000 IRA contribution, only between $1,830 and $1,880 is actually left in the IRA to work for you. The load fund predominated years ago, when funds were sold mainly through brokers and salesmen. But the money market funds helped teach people to use no-load funds (see table 5), where shares are bought directly from the fund.

The load percentage is calculated on the total amount invested. With an 8.5 percent load, $8.50 of every $100 you invest goes to the dealer, while $91.50 actually is applied to purchase shares. In more usual terms, the commission would be figured as $8.50 divided by $91.50, or 9.3 percent.

If you have a brokerage IRA, your broker may recommend load funds as a way of diversifying in the beginning. If the broker gives you careful advice about funds, the advice may turn out to be worth the commission over the long run. But if you are willing and able to do your own research and to use the information sources listed above, there's no need for you to pay a load. As you will see if you study the performance figures, there are more than enough well-managed funds of both types.

If you want more information on funds than you can get from the sources listed in table 5, booklets and lists of funds are available free or at nominal cost from the Investment Company Institute, the general trade association of the mutual fund industry (1775 K St. NW, Washington, DC 20006, [202] 293-7700). Similar information covering no-load funds only is available from the No-Load Mutual Fund Association (Valley Forge, PA 19481, [215] 783-7600).

The multitude of good funds can be a problem in itself. Of the

Table 5
SELECTED MAJOR NO-LOAD MUTUAL FUND GROUPS
(and some of the common stock funds they manage)

Dreyfus Funds
767 Fifth Ave., New York, NY 10153
(800) 223-5525
(Dreyfus Number Nine Fund, Dreyfus Third Century Fund, etc.—also
load funds)

Fidelity Mutual Funds
82 Devonshire St., Boston, MA 02109
(800) 225-6190
(Fidelity Fund, Fidelity Trend Fund, Fidelity Puritan Fund*, etc.)

Financial Programs Funds
P.O. Box 2040, Denver, CO 80201
(800) 525-9831
(Financial Industrial Fund, Financial Industrial Income Fund*, etc.)

Neuberger & Berman Management Funds
342 Madison Ave., New York, NY 10173
(212) 850-8300
(Energy Fund, Guardian Mutual Fund, Partners Fund, etc.)

T. Rowe Price Funds
100 East Pratt St., Baltimore, MD 21202
(800) 638-5660
(T. Rowe Price Growth Stock Fund, T. Rowe Price New Era Fund,
T. Rowe Price New Horizons Fund, etc.)

Scudder Funds
175 Federal St., Boston, MA 02110
(800) 225-2470
(Scudder Common Stock Fund, Scudder Capital Growth Funds, etc.)

Stein Roe & Farnham Funds
150 South Wacker Dr., Chicago, IL 60606
(800) 621-0320
(Stein Roe & Farnham Stock Fund, Stein Roe & Farnham Capital
Opportunities Fund, etc.)

Value Line Funds
711 Third Ave., New York, NY 10017
(800) 223-0818
(Value Line Fund, Value Line Special Situations Fund, etc.)

Vanguard Group
Drummer's Lane, Valley Forge, PA 19482
(800) 523-7025
(Windsor Fund, Wellington Fund*, etc.)

*Income or balanced fund; significant percentage of assets may be in bonds.

350-odd common stock funds in the United States, let's say you have done your homework and narrowed the field down to eight or ten that sound just right for you. Then what? If your IRA is still small, it's hardly sensible to use more than one or two funds. My suggestion is: don't agonize. If fund X and fund Y have had similar performance records in the past, there's no way on earth of predicting which will outperform the other over the next five or ten years. Pick one or two funds arbitrarily out of your own "preferred list" and stay with them for at least a year. You can always put next year's money into different funds, and switch out of your initial choices completely if you wish.

When you find yourself choosing among funds that are roughly equal in quality, consider the advantages of picking a fund that is part of a larger fund *group*. This will give you the convenience of easy switching if you wish to move part or all of your money to a money market fund, a bond fund, or even to a different common stock fund. But the convenience of the fund group shouldn't outweigh performance potential. Several of the finest common stock funds in the country are run by investment managers who concentrate on managing only one or two common stock funds and who have never bothered to expand their operation into a full-fledged group.

SOME SPECIAL FUNDS

With the growth of retirement plans in recent years—not only IRAs but also corporate pension and profit-sharing plans, Keogh plans for the self-employed, and certain other plans—a small but growing number of mutual funds have been formed to serve precisely this market. These funds have investment policies that ignore the income tax considerations of their shareholders, since the shareholders are presumed to be tax-exempt or tax-sheltered.

Does that mean that these funds are right for your IRA? Perhaps. Your choice still has to be based on quality of performance, and all that the tax approach can do is to help performance. Here's why:

The average common stock fund, if it is successful, pays out two types of distributions to its shareholders: ordinary income dividends and long-term capital gains. The shareholder ordinarily

Table 6
TAX-QUALIFIED FUNDS

Name and Address	Type	Assets (millions) 6/30/82	Year Founded	Affiliation
Gintel ERISA Fund Greenwich Office Park, OP-6 Greenwich, CT 06830 (203) 622-6402	No-load	$ 15.4	1982	(a)
Mutual Qualified Income Fund 26 Broadway New York, NY 10004 (212) 908-4048	No-load	13.1	1980	(b)
Partners Fund 342 Madison Ave. New York, NY 10173 (212) 850-8303	No-load	73.9	1968	(c)
Trustees' Commingled Equity Fund Drummer's Lane Valley Forge, PA 19482 (800) 523-7025	No-load	104.7	1980	(d)

a. Companion fund to Gintel Fund.
b. Companion fund to Mutual Shares Corp.
c. Part of Neuberger & Berman Management fund group since 1975.
d. Affiliated with Vanguard fund group.

pays full income tax rates on the income dividends, except for a possible small dividend exclusion. Long-term capital gains, however—gains on securities held for more than one year (as of 1982 regulations)—are taxed basically at only 40 percent of the ordinary rate, and the ability of mutual funds to pass this advantage on to shareholders is one of the great benefits of the mutual fund tax structure. So, unless a common stock fund aims specifically for high income, the portfolio manager will usually make long-term gains the primary target.

There is no doubt that this tax factor does influence a portfolio manager's decisions. If he has held a stock in the fund for six months, for example, and sees good market reasons for selling it at a profit, he has to consider whether to take a short-term gain or to hold the stock past the one-year mark. Or consider the manager who is worried about the market outlook, and thinks it might be wise to sell half of the stocks in his portfolio and put that money into safe, high-yielding U.S. Treasury bills. However, he knows that his shareholders pay full taxes on ordinary income, and that many of them would trade a dollar and a half of current income to get one dollar of long-term capital gains. As a result, he may decide to sell only 25 percent of his stocks, cutting the common stock ratio in the portfolio only to 75 percent, rather than 50 percent. If his original forecast is right, and if the market goes down, he may regret having taken tax problems into account.

The advantage to the manager of one of the *tax-qualified funds* (see table 6), as they are sometimes called, is that he can operate without these inhibitions. So far, so good. If the logic works, the tax-qualified funds should be at the top of the performance ratings. But a lack of tax inhibitions is only one element in investment performance. A good investment manager will do well even if he has to give weight to tax considerations; a poor manager will not be helped much by a lack of inhibitions. There is some evidence that a good manager or management organization will do even better with a tax-qualified fund than with an ordinary common stock fund. But there is also evidence that the policy can go astray. The pioneer fund in this field was The Partners Fund (originally named The Side Fund). Its performance in its early years was disappointing. Then in 1975 it joined a management group with a superior record, and soon it had moved up to a high position in the performance ratings.

So the tax advantage is a real one, but only in the hands of a manager who knows how to use it. It seems safe to predict that several more of these funds will be started in the next few years, particularly by managers who have already established a superior record with one or more regular common stock funds.

Of course, a new tax-qualified fund will not have a long-term performance record to show. But if you like the record of the XYZ Fund, and if the XYZ Group has just started a tax-qualified fund (by whatever title), it is quite reasonable for you to put your IRA dollars in it. However, watch the performance. If the tax-qualified fund doesn't gradually outperform the regular XYZ fund by at least a small margin, then the manager isn't using the tax advantage effectively. And if the general record is disappointing, you should switch out of the tax-qualified fund just as you would out of any other fund that is not performing as you expected.

3

INVESTING IN BONDS AND GOLD

No two investments conjure up more contrasting images than bonds and gold. Bonds are those supposedly stodgy, conservative securities, once beloved by bankers. They are a symbol of trust in the economic system—preserving your dollars and giving you a steady flow of interest payments from now until, in many cases, the year 2000 and beyond. Gold, in contrast, is the last refuge of those who have no trust in the economic system. It is regarded by many as the one sure way of preserving wealth through runaway inflation, economic breakdown, and political chaos.

I have a reason for treating these two investments side by side. To explain why, I will detour back to a point touched on in the previous chapters.

One of the problems in investing today, whether for an IRA or otherwise, is providing for inflation. Certain investments should, as we have discussed, provide some automatic adjustment to inflation. We have seen that short-term market interest rates tend to adjust to the rate of inflation, so that an IRA invested in bank certificates or in a money market fund is likely to grow at least moderately beyond the inflation rate. Common stocks, representing in large part "real" assets, also will tend to adjust for inflation over the long run. Whether inflation accelerates or decelerates, an

IRA invested in either of these two directions should turn out reasonably well.

Bonds and gold won't give you that assurance of adjustment— quite the opposite. The attraction of each of these as an investment depends on a specific inflation forecast. Bonds work well as an investment when the inflation rate is steady or diminishing; gold works best when inflation is roaring. Each can reward you remarkably well under certain economic conditions, but can also cost you heavily if bought at the wrong time or if held for too long.

BONDS

In the days when inflation was negligible, bonds were viewed as a way of avoiding risk. In buying a bond, you in effect lent money for the long term either to the government or to a private corporation. You collected a stated rate of interest for twenty or thirty years, and then got your money back at the maturity date. As a reward for tying up your money for an extended period, you were entitled to a moderately higher interest rate than you would have earned on Treasury bills, commercial paper, or other short-term investments.

All very simple and straightforward. But when inflation began to heat up in the mid-1960s, bonds were dealt a double blow. First, inflation meant that the dollars you were paid back at maturity were worth far less than the dollars you had paid originally for the bond. Second, as interest rates rose, the market prices of old bonds declined with mathematical certainty. If investors could buy new bonds paying, say, 8 percent, they certainly would not pay the full value ("par value" or "face value") for an old 5 percent bond, even if there was no doubt that it would be paid off in full at maturity. So the prices of old bonds (traditionally expressed on the basis of par value as 100) fell from 100 to 80 and then even lower. In the fall of 1981, when the decline appeared at least temporarily to have reached a culmination, old 8 percent U.S. Treasury bonds due in the year 2001 were selling at sixty cents on the dollar, and 7 percent bonds of AT&T due in 2001 were selling at less than fifty-five cents on the dollar.

If you ever make a bad investment and feel stupid about it, remember the insurance companies, banks, pension funds, and other highly sophisticated institutions who held bonds through this twenty-year decline and suffered losses in market value—on paper, at least—amounting to tens of billions of dollars. So much for professional expertise.

As this historical detour makes clear, the attractiveness of bonds depends very much on inflation. When you buy a bond, the interest rate you contract for reflects investors' current expectations regarding inflation. If, in the years after your purchase, inflation turns out to be worse than expected, interest rates will rise, bond prices will fall, and you will not be happy with your bond investment. On the other hand, if the inflation rate drops below expectations, then interest rates should fall and bond prices rise, and all should be well.

The problem is that even the most expert economists have disagreed regularly on inflation forecasts, and most of them have been wrong a good part of the time. You may do better than the experts, but you should think twice before betting on it. The average investor should approach bonds only with great caution; if you do invest in bonds, you should reexamine your assumptions regularly to make sure that conditions are still favorable to your investment.

But I hasten to point out that there is a positive side to the bond picture as well. In the fall of 1981, bond prices sank to record low levels. At that time new corporate bond issues were coming to market with coupons (interest rates) of 16 percent or more. This seemed to reflect investors' predictions—or fears—that inflation in coming years would remain around the peak rates of 11 to 12 percent recorded in 1979 and 1980. Will this be true? Perhaps. But it is worth noting that by mid-1982, the inflation rate had dropped at least temporarily to 6 to 8 percent. If inflation is held within this range for a few years, then bonds carrying interest rates of 14 percent or more will turn out to have been great bargains.

I am forced to leave you with a paradox: bonds can be treacherous, but at certain times they can be outstanding.

If you do want to put part of your IRA money in bonds, how do you go about it? Individual bond issues, like individual stocks, are bought through brokerage firms. (An exception: at times when the U.S. Treasury is selling a new issue of bonds or notes, you can arrange to buy directly through one of the twelve regional Federal Reserve Banks.) Such purchases will be difficult while your IRA is small, since bonds generally sell in $1,000 denominations, and it is usually impractical to buy less than $5,000 or $10,000 of a given bond issue. But there are mutual funds for bonds, just as for stocks, with minimum starting investments from $250 to $500. Or if you have a brokerage IRA, your broker can recommend a variety of closed-end bond funds or bond "unit investment trusts," a different pooling arrangement that allows you to buy relatively small pieces in a pool of new bond issues.

Bond mutual funds operate basically like common stock mutual funds, and you can buy many of them without going through a broker. Performance statistics and lists of names and addresses are available from most of the same sources as for common stock funds (see chapter 2). Most of the major fund groups listed in table 5 have bond funds and will be glad to send you information. Pick a fund with good total performance over the last few years; it doesn't have to be the one with the highest current yield. Review your investment regularly.

Just as with common stock funds, there are *load* (commission) and *no-load* bond mutual funds. If you have a brokerage IRA, commissions on closed-end funds are the same as on other publicly traded stocks; commissions on unit investment trusts are generally somewhat higher.

There is a special type of bond called *zero-coupon bonds* that you will be hearing more about, and which may be useful for your IRA. Zero-coupon bonds are so called because they pay no interest during the life of the bond. The interest is compounded, cumulated, and paid off in one lump-sum payment at maturity. There is a reason for this. Let's say you buy an ordinary twenty-year bond with a 12 percent coupon. Most bonds pay interest semiannually, so the interest will be paid out to you at the rate of 6 percent every six months. If you bought the bond in order to have spendable income, that's fine. But in an IRA, you can't take out dividends or interest—they must be reinvested. A few years from now, if interest rates drop, your bond will continue to pay 12 percent, but you may be reinvesting the interest payments at only 8 or 10 percent, and you will find that your bond investment is actually compounding at less than the 12 percent rate.

A zero-coupon bond solves that problem. For example, in early 1982 you could have bought a zero-coupon bond of BankAmerica Corp. due in November 1992, with a face value of $1,000, but priced at only $250. When the bond pays off in 1992 at $1,000, the investors will have received a return of over 13 percent compounded annually on their original $250 investment, irrespective of how interest rates may have changed in the interim.

So the zero-coupon bond not only locks in a certain return for a certain number of years, but locks it in *fully compounded.* For a taxable account, there are drawbacks, because the bondholder must pay income tax on the annual interest accruals even though no dollars are actually received. But the arrangement is ideal for your nontaxable IRA.

Because of the more complete commitment to a particular interest rate, zero-coupon bonds should fluctuate in price more widely than ordinary bonds. If interest rates drop after you buy a zero-coupon bond, it should rise to more of a premium in price than an old-style bond issued at the same time. On the other hand, if you buy a zero-coupon bond and interest rates subsequently rise, your bond will probably drop more sharply in price than an ordinary bond.

If you trust your judgment enough to buy bonds, there's no reason why you shouldn't make the commitment more complete by buying zero-coupon bonds. Brokerage firms have set up arrangements so that you can buy into a pool of zero-coupon bonds in small pieces tailored in size to fit your IRA (see chapter 4). As your IRA grows larger, you can also buy zero-coupon bonds directly, but the unit trust arrangement may still carry advantages in flexibility and diversification.

A further note: What if you like the concept of zero-coupon bonds but hesitate to move away from government-guaranteed investments? Don't give up hope: the U.S. Treasury is said to be thinking of issuing zero-coupon government bonds. Also, by the time this book appears, the banks will be offering zero-coupon certificates that qualify for the FDIC guarantee on bank deposits.

In this chapter, I have talked only about high-quality bonds (U.S. government obligations and prime corporates), where the only risks are market risks relating to interest rate movements. There are also lower-quality corporate issues, where you incur the additional risk that the corporation may not be able to pay interest or repay principal on schedule. These bonds are best left to the experts; if you buy into a mutual fund that invests in such issues, make sure the manager has a long and successful track record.

GOLD

Now that I have presented the warnings appropriate for bonds, what about gold?

Gold has been a measure and store of value since ancient times, and there is a whole class of investors and investment advisers—known collectively as the "goldbugs"—who regard gold as the outstanding or even the only valid long-term investment.

Indeed, the gold market has shown a remarkable ability to survive wars, political upheavals, and the attempts of politicians to control it. But does this mean that you should invest in gold for your IRA? I have my doubts. But since gold investments may be recommended to you, let's briefly put gold in perspective.

The gold boom of the 1970s was a catch-up phenomenon—compensation for the long period from 1933 to the 1960s, when governments successfully held gold at an official price of $35 per ounce in pursuit of monetary stability. By 1971, this controlled price no longer could be held, and the market price of gold caught up rapidly with the whole postwar inflation, rising close to $200 per ounce in 1974 and soaring to a speculative peak of $875 in early 1980. The market then settled back, and by early 1982 gold was down to $300–$400.

In this range, even after the decline from the peak, gold was still selling for ten times the official price that had governed the market until 1970, representing a gain over twelve years at a rate of more than 20 percent compounded annually. But don't forget all those years when the price was stuck at $35. Over the whole postwar period, the rise in the price of gold works out to a gain of only about 7 percent compounded annually, before adjusting for inflation—well below the gain of 10.8 percent compounded annually that, as we saw in chapter 2, was achieved by an average investment in common stocks.

The postwar price history teaches two simple, useful lessons about gold. First, over the long term gold does adjust to inflation. If you expect runaway inflation in the United States—and this is behind the thinking of some of the goldbugs—then gold might be an excellent investment.

Second, gold can fluctuate sharply in price due to political fears, the threat of inflation, and a host of speculative factors. If you succumb to crowd psychology and buy gold when it is at a speculative peak, as it was in late 1979 and early 1980, it may take you years to get even, unless we actually get that runaway inflation you were presumably worried about.

How do you know whether the price of gold is reasonable? Economists have tried to determine this "reasonable" price by measuring the price of gold historically against the price of other commodities. On this basis, a reasonable price for gold in early 1982 might perhaps have been in the $250–$350 range. And if that were true—and remember that no one can be sure—then the actual gold market was not far out of line.

Given the above background, what should you actually do about gold investments? I would do without them. I don't see any convincing evidence that the United States is headed for runaway inflation. And as I have pointed out previously, you can protect against moderate inflation over the long run by investing in common stocks, money market funds, or bank certificates.

But if you can't sleep because of fears of inflation, then having some gold in your IRA may be preferable to taking sleeping pills. In that case, let me urge you to have the courage to buy gold when it is out of favor and no one is recommending it—that is, when the price is low—not when it is booming, the price is already high, and all your friends assure you that it is bound to go up another 50 percent.

Table 7
FUNDS INVESTING PRIMARILY IN GOLD STOCKS

Name	Type	Assets (millions) 12/31/81	Year Founded
ASA Ltd.	Closed-end	$527	1958
Fidelity Select Portfolios: Precious Metals & Minerals Portfolio	No-load	1	1981
*Golconda Investors Ltd.	No-load	8	1958
International Investors	Load	276	†1968
*Lexington Goldfund	No-load	1	1979
*Precious Metals Holdings	Closed-end	67	1974
Research Capital Fund	Load	54	†1973
Strategic Investments Fund	Load	29	1974
United Services Gold Shares	No-load	89	†1974

*Significant percentage of assets can be in gold bullion.
†Year fund began to concentrate in gold stocks.

How do you actually go about investing in gold? The IRA rules were changed in 1982 and now forbid buying gold or other metals directly for your IRA. But even if you could put gold bullion in your IRA, the metal earns no income; you can accomplish much the same purpose by investing in shares of the companies that mine gold. The higher-quality companies own substantial gold reserves, and by owning the shares, you indirectly own an interest in the metal.

If you wish to select gold-mining shares yourself, or with the help of a broker, you can do so through a brokerage IRA (see chapter 4). But here, as in the common stock field, it may be best to leave the choice of individual issues to professionals, and you should make use of one of the mutual funds that specialize in gold-mining shares. Some of these funds are shown in table 7.

International Investors, the largest of the gold funds, was the leading performer among all mutual funds in the decade 1971–80, rising 1,075 percent (with dividends reinvested), which works out to an average compounded gain of 28 percent annually. Incidentally, this included a gain of 177 percent in 1979 alone, followed by another gain of 65 percent in 1980. But in 1981, International Investors dropped 19 percent. If excitement is what you crave, the gold funds probably won't disappoint you.

Notice that the funds listed in the table include both load and no-load mutual funds. I have also listed two closed-end funds that can't be bought directly but can be bought if you have a brokerage IRA. More details on the performance of all of these funds are available in the fund performance sources listed in chapter 2. A few of the funds have policies permitting the holding of gold bullion as a part of assets, which may or may not help their performance over the long run.

What if you don't crave excitement, but simply want to manage your IRA intelligently for the best possible results? Some professional investment managers think it makes perfectly good sense to have 5 to 10 percent of one's assets in gold shares, as part of a balanced investment approach and as a hedge against inflation. If you want to add a moderate interest in gold to your IRA, once it has grown enough so that you can comfortably diversify, I won't argue with you.

But if you are speculating, at least speculate intelligently: try to buy your gold shares when the gold market is depressed, the price of gold is low, and all your friends are buying something else.

4

INVESTING WITH BROKERAGE FIRMS AND INSURANCE COMPANIES

BROKERAGE FIRM IRAS

Most of the larger brokerage firms offer what has become known as a "self-directed" IRA. Here you have virtually the same wide choice of investments as in a regular brokerage account—stocks, bonds, mutual funds, and several less familiar choices. Most of these can be bought, sold, or switched by means of a simple telephone call to your individual broker. For choice and flexibility of investments, the brokerage IRA easily outdistances competing IRAs.

But a brokerage IRA is not for everyone. The opportunities for choice also provide you with the opportunity to make mistakes, some of which can be serious and costly. The fees and commissions in a brokerage IRA are also likely to be substantially higher than in the other types of IRAs we have surveyed. Still, a brokerage IRA makes sense for certain specific people.

First and foremost, the brokerage IRA is for the experienced investor who knows how to choose his or her own investments. If this description fits you, then I don't need to give you much advice. But before you open an IRA with your regular brokerage firm, make sure its IRA fees are not too far out of line with those of other brokerage firms.

Second, perhaps you are not an experienced investor yourself, but you want the range of choice of a brokerage IRA and you know an individual broker whom you trust and respect. In that case, it's reasonable to let him (or her) advise you on your IRA.

Third, you may want to open a brokerage IRA not for flexibility, but because you want to put your IRA in one or more of the specific investments available only through a brokerage IRA—for example, a real estate limited partnership, or a special mutual fund offered only by a particular brokerage firm. In that case, I hope you have done your research well, and carefully considered the alternatives discussed in this book.

Finally, perhaps I have convinced you that you should have common stock investments in your IRA, but you need to talk to someone periodically for reassurance and advice. Some no-load mutual funds have people available to give you that kind of help, but others do not. A broker may be the answer. While your IRA is still small, the broker's function may be simply to help you choose a good mutual fund. He will probably sell you a "load" fund on which you will pay a commission, and your total fees will certainly be higher than if you had done your own research and gone directly to a no-load fund. If the broker gives you good advice, you will be better off over the long run than if you had done a mediocre job of selection on your own. However, a word of warning: if you are in this situation, I suggest picking a brokerage firm that does *not* sponsor its own mutual funds. The temptation for a broker to recommend an in-house fund is substantial, and the impartial advice you are looking for may not be there.

Be extremely careful about relying on an individual broker's advice unless you have good reason to trust his or her skill and quality. Am I advising you against walking into a reputable brokerage firm and relying on whichever individual broker is assigned to you? Yes, I am. The average broker (technically, they are called registered representatives) may be an honest, hard-working professional. But investing is a strange art that stubbornly resists being reduced to a science. As we saw in studying mutual funds, professional investors, like amateurs, can range from excellent to poor in their results. While you can easily compare mutual funds on the basis of published performance records, there are no such data available to help you rate a brokerage firm or an individual broker. Even if a firm is completely reputable, you don't know whether its individual brokers will give you good investment advice or not. So unless you intend to choose securities yourself, or know a particular broker who has consistently done well for his or her clients, you will be leaving less to chance if you do your own research and select one or more mutual funds for your IRA, as explained in chapter 2.

Another reason for caution is that your IRA will, from the broker's point of view, inevitably be a small account in the early years. Brokers are only human—they generally work on commissions, and they will allocate their time to their profit. A successful broker isn't likely to spend much time on your new IRA unless he has a broader relationship with you or unless he has specifically decided to allocate extra time to developing IRA business for the future. In the early years, he can solve this problem by recommending that your IRA be invested in mutual funds. But I again note that you will save costs if you are able to do this selection job yourself.

I will have more to say later about the costs of a brokerage IRA. But first, let's turn to the more important question of the investments that this type of IRA opens up to you.

Here are a few things that you are *not* permitted to do. You are not permitted to borrow in your IRA, so you can't buy securities on *margin*, which is simply a form of borrowing in order to buy more securities than you could otherwise. That also rules out commodity futures trading, and certain limited partnership deals in which the partnership borrows, either by mortgaging real estate or otherwise.

Your brokerage firm may have its own additional restrictions ruling out certain transactions that it considers too speculative for an IRA. And, of course, there are some investments that by their nature are simply not suitable for an IRA. It's pointless, for example, to pay extra for investments that carry a tax advantage, since your IRA is nontaxable until money is distributed to you. That rules out all tax-exempt bonds. It also means that preferred stocks, which carry a tax advantage for corporations seeking income, probably will not be a good choice for your IRA; if you want long-term, fixed-income securities, you will do better with bonds. And be wary of any investment that is usually recommended for its tax-sheltering qualities.

What about the things that you *can* do with a brokerage IRA? Your choices will of course depend on your own situation and preferences, but here are some of the possibilities.

Common Stocks Enough was said about common stocks in chapter 2, so I will only repeat that common stocks, if expertly selected, can be highly rewarding. (We have agreed, I think, that it is pointless to put tax-shelter-type investments in your IRA. I now find that some financial writers recommend against buying long-term growth stocks for an IRA, arguing that an IRA doesn't benefit from the favorable tax treatment of long-term capital gains. This involves a misconception of what common stocks are all about. As pointed out in chapter 2, common stocks have outperformed most other securities investments over the long term on a "total return" basis, without any reference to the tax advantage. The tax advantage gives you one more reason for stressing common stocks in a taxable account, but the basic rationale for buying common stocks as a long-term investment is valid irrespective of tax considerations.)

Bonds In your brokerage IRA, you have a wide choice of U.S. Treasury bonds, U.S. government agency obligations, a multitude of corporate issues, and various types of bond funds. Note what was said in chapter 3 about zero-coupon bonds. Brokerage firms have been putting zero-coupon bonds into convenient packages called *unit investment trusts*—pools of securities that resemble a closed-end fund (see below) but in which the list of securities is fixed at the beginning and stays the same throughout. You can buy shares in this pool in relatively small denominations. The commission will probably be higher than if you bought the bonds directly, but if the sponsor of the trust is reputable, the convenience and diversification are probably worth the extra outlay.

Writing Call Options Since investments that yield high income carry no tax disadvantages in an IRA, many brokers will help you manage a program to generate extra income by buying common stocks and writing (selling) *call options* against them. This

48

means that you sell to some other investor the right to purchase ("call") your stock at a specified price (the "striking price") for a specified period of time. The premium you are paid for the option is extra income to you, but you give up the opportunity for any substantial capital gain because if the market price of your stock rises above the striking price, the holder of the option will exercise the right to buy the stock. The stocks you buy still have to be well chosen—if your stock drops sharply in price, the small premium you earned by selling a call option will only partly offset the damage. (In a taxable account, writing call options has tax consequences that we need not consider here.)

Trading Options Writing a call option against a stock you own is a conservative technique for generating extra income; *buying* a call option (or *put option*), on the other hand, is highly speculative, since you are betting that the price of the stock will go up (or down) within a specified time. If the stock price doesn't move the way you expect, the option will decline sharply in price or become completely worthless. Many brokerage firms will not permit you to *buy* puts or calls in an IRA, but you can find one or two that will accommodate you if you are determined to live dangerously.

Closed-end Funds A brokerage IRA gives you the opportunity to enter the world of *closed-end funds*—funds that have issued a fixed number of shares. (As we saw in chapter 2, mutual funds are "open-end" funds that stand ready to issue or redeem shares on demand.) To buy into a closed-end fund, you don't buy new shares from the fund; instead, you buy shares in the open market from another investor who wishes to sell. Such major closed-end stock funds as Tri-Continental Corp. and Lehman Corp. have been in business for a long time. In recent years, there has been a growth of closed-end bond funds. Often shares of closed-end funds can be bought in the open market at a discount from their underlying net asset value (that is, the aggregate market value of the securities they own). But just as the market price may provide you with a discount when you buy, so you may have to accept a discount when you sell. However, the possibility that the discount may narrow after you buy your shares opens up an extra opportunity for capital gains.

Real Estate Your brokerage IRA permits buying securities of several types of companies in the real estate field. Many of these companies have experienced severe difficulties since the speculative real estate excesses of the early 1970s. Accordingly, the field is an interesting one for expert bargain hunters, but it is hardly for novices. Among the companies that can be interesting for an IRA are the *real estate investment trusts* (REITs). They can pass net real estate income through to their shareholders without double taxation, much like the arrangement by which a mutual fund passes through dividends and capital gains to its holders. Brokers have also begun offering interests in limited partnerships designed to generate high income from real estate investments, usually with some potential for capital appreciation as well. These differ from the more familiar limited partnerships tailored for high-bracket taxpayers, which are programmed to generate the maximum in tax write-offs and the minimum in taxable income.

Oil and Gas Your brokerage IRA gives you access to all publicly traded oil and gas securities, from the small exploration companies to the giant internationals. Ask your broker for information on the small number of oil royalty trusts traded on the exchanges (for example, Houston Oil Trust and Mesa Royalty Trust). The trust form of organization permits a pass-through of income, which benefits your IRA. You are also likely to encounter *limited partnerships* intended to produce high income from oil and gas properties, and these may be particularly suited to IRAs and other tax-exempt accounts.

A word of advice about limited partnerships: whether these are in real estate, oil, equipment leasing, or something else, don't buy into them just because you like the glamour of the name. The limited partnership has certain unique advantages when the object is to pass through losses and other tax deductions to investors. Passing through income is a somewhat different matter. While the limited partnership can pass through income without double taxation, so can the REITs and oil trusts mentioned above. Note that these publicly traded trusts can be bought for a usual stock exchange commission, while limited partnership interests are likely to be offered with an underwriting commission of 8 percent or more. Before you buy limited partnership interests for your IRA, ask your broker to review the possible alternatives.

The whole subject of fees and commissions in a brokerage IRA deserves your attention. According to the schedules currently posted, it will cost you from $20 to $30 to open a brokerage IRA, and the annual maintenance charge is between $25 and $50. If you are buying only mutual funds, these charges may be lower. But beware of custodial arrangements that impose a high fee for terminations or switching out of the IRA, and also be careful of custodian fees based on the *value* of your account, which may work out to be small in the early years but sizable later on. Many brokerage firms do not specify any minimum for your starting IRA investment. But considering the start-up and maintenance fees, it will hardly make sense for you to open a brokerage IRA unless you can invest the full $2,000 annually, or close to it.

There will also be *commission* charges on most of your individual purchase and sale transactions. Commission charges on small purchases or sales of a common stock (say $1,000 or so) may be about 3 percent of the amount involved; commissions on load mutual funds, on special partnership interests, or on unit trusts may be as high as 8 or 9 percent of the purchase price. To justify these charges, you had better obtain good results.

On the subject of commissions, consider another point. Most people think of brokers in terms of the large "full-service" firms such as Merrill Lynch, Shearson/American Express, E. F. Hutton, Bache, Paine Webber, and Dean Witter Reynolds, to name a few. But there are also "discount brokers," which provide little or no research or advice but will execute your stock and bond trades for substantially lower commissions. (They may *not* be able to save you money on special offerings and underwritings such as limited partnership interests, since in these cases the commission is usually fixed by the terms of the offering.) If you intend to manage your own IRA, don't need a broker's advice, and expect to buy and sell stocks and/or bonds actively, look for the advertisements of the discount brokers in the Sunday *New York Times*, *Barron's*, and similar publications. Certain of the larger discount brokers have already advertised IRAs. The fees to open and maintain an IRA at a discount brokerage firm will be about the same as at a full-service firm, but you will save on commissions.

The fact that the discount brokers are generally smaller and not so well established isn't necessarily a major obstacle. For one thing, most brokerage plans appoint a bank as custodian. But since the securities are usually still left on deposit at the broker's, the ultimate protection lies in the fact that brokerage accounts are insured up to $500,000 by the Securities Investor Protection Corp. (SIPC), which has been a blessing to brokerage customers since it was established in 1970. Make sure your brokerage firm is a member (most are legally required to be), and verify that any unusual investments recommended by the broker are covered under the SIPC protection. And what if your IRA grows beyond $500,000? Well, let's hope that by then the SIPC limit will have been raised.

Whether your IRA is at a full-service or a discount broker, the combined fees and commissions will look relatively large in the early years when the total dollars in your IRA are still small. Mutual funds are the most likely answer to this problem. If the brokerage firm of your choice has a low-fee arrangement for buying mutual funds only, you can, as previously discussed, start your IRA that way and switch to a fully self-directed IRA later on. Or, with a little extra effort, you can start your IRA directly with any no-load mutual fund of your choice, or even with a bank, and then do a complete switch to a brokerage IRA after a few years, when the size of your IRA justifies the change.

To sum up: only you can judge whether you or your broker has the judgment and experience for a brokerage IRA. Certainly a brokerage IRA gives you the maximum investment flexibility. If this advantage is used well enough, it can readily justify the higher cost of a brokerage IRA.

There is another point that perhaps doesn't deserve to be weighed in the decision but that still can't be denied: managing your own investments can be *fun*. There are few activities more interesting and satisfying than investment management. It makes you think not only about your own financial position but also about what is going on in the world. The possibilities for research and study are endless. The new IRA law could create a whole new class of savers/investors, and I have no doubt that many of them will eventually be attracted to the challenge and interest of a self-directed IRA.

Who should *not* have a brokerage IRA? In my opinion, even the experienced person should be wary of this arrangement if he or she will not have time to think about it regularly. And to the novice who wants to learn more about investing, I advise caution—it's remarkably easy to lose money on misguided investments, especially if you are swayed by popular fads. If you want to move out of the novice stage, don't learn at your own expense. Put your IRA in a mutual fund or bank, read some books on investing, take a few evening courses, see if your judgment seems to work out well, and then, when you are ready, switch into a self-directed IRA.

INSURANCE COMPANY IRAS

The life insurance companies have fallen behind the banks and brokers in promoting IRA plans. However, life insurance companies are giant institutions with tens of thousands of sales agents scattered across the country, and they are not about to neglect the expanding IRA market.

But whether the insurance companies deserve your hard-earned IRA dollars is questionable. Based on their initial offerings, the typical IRA annuity that a life insurance company is likely to recommend is, from an investment point of view, much like a bank IRA. You are offered a guaranteed rate of return for a relatively short period of time (a year, for example), but with no guarantee of what the rate will be on renewal, or what rate will be available on next year's contribution. The assured long-term return that one might expect from an insurance program simply isn't there.

That isn't really surprising. The insurance companies, like the rest of us, have no accurate way of forecasting what interest rates will be ten or twenty years down the road. And they are in the business of taking risks only when the risks are measurable.

What you can be certain of is that the fees and/or commissions charged on an insurance IRA will be higher than those charged by a bank—and the rates of return offered may be lower. A life insurance agent will probably be willing to call on you, sit down, and make the initial paperwork on your IRA simple and painless. But his time has to be compensated, and his compensation is built into the industry's pricing structure. If you are willing to lose a few dollars to pay for the extra help and convenience, that's up to you. But you will probably find that the banks and money market funds can give you most of the same features as an insurance IRA, and at lower cost.

This is really not a new situation. For many years, experts have warned consumers that the long-term savings programs offered by the life insurance industry are a poor value relative to the competition. That's why many people buy only *term* life insurance—pure life insurance, without any savings element—preferring to put their savings dollars elsewhere. Since your IRA is completely a savings program—no part of it is permitted to go for actual life insurance—the insurance industry may have to come up with some changes or innovations in this area if they are to be competitive.

Your insurance agent may recommend a contract that combines an IRA annuity with life insurance, but you will only be able to take a tax deduction on the portion of the premium that pays for the annuity and *not* for the life insurance. The company will provide the information for this breakdown, but the whole arrangement will reduce the flexibility of your IRA, and I can't recommend it. If you need life insurance, buy the insurance separately.

The insurance IRAs do have at least two additional features that are somewhat distinctive. An insurance company can provide you at retirement with a true life annuity as an option—regular payments that last for your lifetime, or for the combined joint lifetimes of you and your spouse. Since banks are not in the business of betting on how long you will live, most bank plans—and other IRA plans using a bank as custodian or trustee—only offer a payout over a fixed number of years.

This difference is not really a difference, since at retirement you can arrange for your bank custodian or trustee to apply the balance in your account to buy an annuity contract for you from an insurance company that qualifies as an "individual retirement annuity." The effect is then the same as if you had had an insurance IRA. You are not taxed on the lump sum applied to purchase the contract, but only on the annuity payments as you receive them.

A warning: keep in mind that a life annuity may be a poor bargain in any case. An annuity is generally intended to provide lifetime income for you (or you and your spouse), with little or nothing left for your heirs. At 1982 interest rates, you could probably buy a high-quality, long-term corporate bond that would provide the same income flow to you for twenty or thirty years, with the bond passing intact to your estate in case of death.

Another feature of most insurance IRAs is that you can arrange (for an additional premium) to have the company continue your investment program in case of disability. In effect, this adds disability insurance to your IRA. If disability insurance is a wise idea for you, I suggest that you plan it in relation to your total financial picture and buy it separately. There is no need to limit the flexibility of your IRA.

The built-in life annuity and the disability provision should be regarded only as convenience features, because they can be duplicated elsewhere with a little effort, and with a probable saving in costs. Convenience is fine, but your choice of an IRA investment should be governed by its ultimate dollar potential.

Based on 1982 indications, the interest rate you earn for any period in an insurance IRA is likely to be less than you would be earning at a bank or money fund. You will almost certainly also incur higher fees. Apart from the annual maintenance fee, there may be special fees payable when it is time for your money to be distributed, and substantial penalties if you switch out of the insurance IRA at an early date. The starting date for withdrawals in some policies is later than age fifty-nine and a half, cutting your flexibility further.

A final word: for some people, the attraction of an insurance company savings program is the discipline of having to make regular payments. I know very well how easy it is to delay putting money aside. But in an IRA, there are better ways of dealing with this problem.

First, you *know* that you will only get your tax deduction for the year if you make your contribution ($2,000 or whatever you can afford) by the time your tax return is due. Most people will find this discipline enough. But if not, you can set up your own automatic payment plan. Almost all banks will be glad to make monthly or even weekly deductions from your checking or savings account for an IRA. Many mutual funds have arrangements letting you authorize your bank to make automatic monthly or quarterly payments to the fund for your IRA plan. Or your employer may set up an automatic payroll deduction plan (see appendix B). If it's convenience you want, you can get it from several sponsors. But convenience won't make you rich. Keep your eye on the ball and concentrate on building up those dollars for retirement.

II

MANAGING YOUR IRA FOR A SECURE FUTURE

5

HOW TO SWITCH, DIVERSIFY, AND ROLL OVER YOUR INVESTMENTS

No matter how carefully and intelligently you have chosen the initial investment or investments for your IRA, your work isn't over—far from it. The key to successful investing is to remember that you live in a changing world, and that you must also change.

If you want your IRA to do the most for you, then on a regular basis—at least once a year, but preferably far more often than that—take time to *think* about your IRA. Review what you have contributed and how it is invested. Consider whether the investments have earned or developed as you expected. Then ask yourself the following questions:

1. Am I satisfied with the way I have handled my IRA?

2. Has there been any change in the factors I considered when I picked the investments that are now in my IRA?

3. If I were starting fresh today, would I choose the investments that I now have in my IRA?

The last question is the most important, because it lets you know whether you have answered the other questions honestly. If you would choose your investments differently today than when you last arranged them, think things through carefully. Is there a good reason for your change in preference? If so, then it is time to change the investments in your IRA.

TIME FOR A CHANGE

There are many reasons for rearranging your investments in an IRA. I will cite only a few examples.

First, your economic situation may have changed. Perhaps your dollars have built up in a brokerage IRA or a common stock fund. Now you expect to retire in a year or two, and you want to cut your risks and lock in the dollars you now have. The natural solution is to switch to a money market fund or bank IRA.

Or perhaps you started your IRA with a local savings bank. You have many years to go before retirement. You have been watching and studying common stock funds and have decided to switch part of your IRA into one or two funds with excellent long-term growth records.

The reasons for change may not be in your own situation but in outside economic conditions. Perhaps you kept your IRA dollars in a money market fund while interest rates were high, but rates are coming down and a broker you know can help you do better. Maybe you put the funds in an aggressive common stock fund and have done so well that you suspect common stocks are now overpriced. Perhaps the economy looks so bad that you want the safety of a government securities money market fund.

Any of the factors that caused you to choose an investment may have changed. You may also need to make a change simply because you have made a mistake—one of your choices hasn't worked out the way you expected. If the reasons for your original choice no longer seem convincing, and you have thought your situation through carefully, by all means make whatever changes are necessary to get your IRA dollars invested where you now think they should be.

I am not suggesting change for the sake of change, but the *willingness* to make changes is essential to anyone who wants to make his or her investments perform best.

The average person, unfortunately, often stays with an investment long after its attraction has faded. You may hold on out of inertia or fear—the fear of making a mistake, or of taking a loss. Inaction can be expensive. Discipline yourself to make changes promptly when they are required.

People sometimes hesitate to change investments because they feel committed to a particular broker, fund representative, or institution. Don't put yourself in that position. Loyalty to people and principles is admirable. Loyalty to investments can be an expensive error. So be professional—make careful judgments and follow them through.

There's one technical point that you should be aware of. I have been telling you not to be inhibited about making investment changes in your IRA. In an ordinary investment account, one of the inhibiting factors is the capital gains tax—the tax that you pay when an investment is sold at a profit. But in your IRA, there's no capital gains tax to pay, and you can ignore taxes completely when considering changing investments. Sell an investment in your IRA whenever there is a basic reason to be out of that investment and into something better.

SPREADING YOUR RISKS

As a good manager, there's another kind of change that you will want to consider as your IRA grows—diversification.

Why diversification? Isn't the trick simply to pick the one best investment?

Of course—if there were any way to be certain which is the best. But this is an uncertain world; investing is far from an exact science, and even with the most careful thinking and planning— even with complete alertness to changing conditions—there is no way to be *sure* that a particular investment is the right one. The solution is to diversify—to include different investments in your IRA, striking a balance that will let your IRA perform well under any conceivable condition.

In the first two or three years, when your IRA is small, diversification may seem like more trouble than it's worth. But the bigger your IRA, the more reason to consider varying your investments.

Diversification may not involve any actual switching of investments. Let's say, for example, that you have put $2,000 a year into a money market fund for the first two years. You might reasonably decide to leave that investment in place, but to put your next year's contribution in a common stock fund.

The law gives you complete flexibility in this respect. As stated earlier, you can have as many separate IRAs as you want, as long as your combined contributions to all of them don't exceed the annual limit. You can contribute to all of them each year, or only to one and not to the others, or in any mixture and proportion you want. Of course, individual sponsors may set minimum amounts that you can invest at any one time in their particular plans, but you always have the choice of contributing nothing at all (in most accounts), and you can ordinarily let an IRA accumulate indefinitely without new contributions.

Diversification involves striking a balance that fits your own preferences and objectives, and no simple rule can hold for all individuals. For example, I have stressed the attraction of common stock investments for the long term, and I can imagine conditions when you might be comfortable with an IRA invested exclusively in a selection of common stocks or common stock funds. But if common stock prices have been rising for two or three years, and you are afraid that the next move may be downward, you may decide to shift part of your dollars to a money market fund. Or you may feel that all forecasts are suspect and that you want to be permanently diversified—say 50 percent in common stock funds; 25 percent in a money market fund; and the balance in some combination of a bond fund, gold fund, and perhaps some other kind of investment. The possibilities are limitless; strike a balance that is comfortable for you.

If you have other investments besides your IRA, you should think of your total investment picture. In this case, use the IRA tax advantage effectively. If you want your investment program to include some long-term growth stocks and some fixed-income investments, and you don't need high current income to spend, put the stocks primarily in your regular account, where you will benefit from the tax advantage of long-term gains, and concentrate the fixed-income investments in your IRA, where the interest income will be sheltered from taxes.

HOW TO MOVE YOUR DOLLARS

Now that we have talked about switching and diversifying, let's discuss briefly how to go about it.

Diversifying is easy. As indicated above, you can open as many different IRAs as you want, as long as your *combined* annual contributions don't exceed the annual limit. If you own shares in a mutual fund that is part of a fund group, there is usually a provision for easy diversification within the group—often it can be done with a telephone call. And if you have a brokerage IRA, the whole arrangement is aimed at easy diversification, with most different types of investments available through a simple telephone call to your broker.

Switching completely out of one investment and into another is almost as simple. But your ability to switch freely may be curtailed by your choice of sponsor. That's why I have urged you to think carefully before committing your IRA dollars to bank certificates or insurance programs that penalize early withdrawals.

With a brokerage IRA, switching is only a matter of a phone call. Switches within a mutual fund group are almost as simple, with arrangements for telephone switching now becoming widespread.

But if you are switching from one sponsor to another, you have to work a little harder. IRA plans allow for switching to a new plan with a different custodian, but your old custodian will want instructions in writing. So write a letter as follows:

(Date)

ABC Bank
(Address)

Re: (Your name)
(Your present IRA account number)

Dear Sirs:

I have established an IRA under the *(name of fund, bank, etc.)* Plan, for which the XYZ Bank *(new bank's name and address)* acts as custodian. Please transfer the assets from the above account directly to the XYZ Bank as custodian.

Very truly yours,
(Signature)

(Signature guarantee
if required)

You can of course specify that only part of the assets be transferred out of your old account. And if you are making a transfer from a bank IRA, and are waiting for a certain certificate or certificates to mature, your letter should instruct that the transfer only be made at maturity. Your custodian may require that your signature on the letter be guaranteed by your commercial bank or by a recognized brokerage firm.

Send a copy of this letter to your new plan sponsor. If you haven't received a confirmation of the switch within ten days, telephone both your old sponsor or custodian and your new sponsor and ask them to follow through on the transaction. Since banks are often less prompt when sending money out than when taking it in, it's wise to keep after your old custodian until you know the switch has been completed. Some switches will require a processing fee—it should only be $5 or $10. Check the switching fee amount before you join a sponsor's IRA.

ROLLOVERS

The subject of rollovers can be confusing. The word *rollover* has two different meanings for an IRA, and often the distinction is not made clear.

The first type of rollover, which I will call a *true rollover,* has nothing to do with the kind of switching between investments that we have just been discussing. It refers to a procedure that can be followed by an individual who receives a lump-sum distribution from an employer's pension or profit-sharing plan. Instead of taking this distribution and paying taxes on it, the individual is generally permitted to *roll over* the distribution tax-free into a special IRA—usually designated by some such term as *special rollover account.*

As you can see, this type of rollover has nothing to do with managing investments in your regular IRA. The rules for true rollovers will be discussed in detail in appendix C.

The second type of rollover I will refer to as a *switch rollover,* since it involves a transfer of assets from one regular IRA to another. The rules provide that you can withdraw part or all of the assets from an IRA and not be taxed on the proceeds, as long as you deposit the proceeds in another regular IRA within sixty days.

(Of course, you do *not* get a tax deduction for the amount switched to the new IRA).

A switch rollover takes place only when the IRA assets are *paid out to you* before being redeposited in another IRA. When the transfer is made directly from one custodian or trustee to another, under the procedure we discussed above, no rollover has technically taken place.

This distinction is important, because a switch rollover is permitted in your IRA only once a year. Once you have completed such a rollover, you must wait at least a year before doing it again. By contrast, there's no limit on how often you can make direct transfers from one custodian/trustee to another custodian/trustee. Remember this point, since some sponsors either don't understand it or don't explain it adequately.

So there's usually no reason to use the switch rollover procedure. But it's worth keeping the rules in mind. If a sponsor or custodian/trustee should misunderstand your instructions and send your IRA dollars out to you by mistake, you have no tax problem as long as the money is back in an IRA within sixty days.

But be careful! The sixty-day limit is final and inflexible. Many custodians or trustees automatically file a report with the IRS regarding any direct distribution to a planholder, and you *must* be prepared to prove to the IRS that the distribution was rolled over within the time limit if you want to avoid being taxed on the amount distributed.

There may be a rare case where you intentionally take the money out of your IRA, use it briefly for some special purpose, and then put it back in an IRA before the sixty days are up. I have heard of one case of a man who desperately needed cash to complete a real estate closing while he was still waiting for his mortgage application to be approved. Fortunately, he had a large sum in a special rollover IRA. He withdrew the cash, completed the deal, then got his mortgage and put back the IRA money, all within sixty days. He certainly deserves an award for creative financing. But considering all the foolish things that one can do with money within sixty days, I suggest that IRA dollars are best left with the custodians and trustees—and the less you see of those dollars, the better.

6

MAKING THE PENALTY TAX WORK FOR YOU

What if you want to take money out of your IRA before you reach the age of fifty-nine and a half? The answer: not only do you pay ordinary income taxes on the withdrawal, you also pay a penalty tax, fixed at a *flat 10 percent* of the amount withdrawn.

The word *penalty* has a chilling effect on most people, and the words *penalty tax* invoke a double chill. Many people will hesitate to put money in an IRA if they think that they may have to take it out before retirement.

You don't have to be overly cautious. The penalty is really a very modest one and should not prevent you from putting money in an IRA unless you *know* that you will need the cash within two or three years.

Why do I minimize the penalty? You may be surprised at how quickly the tax advantages of an IRA will offset the 10 percent tax penalty—nowhere is the miracle of tax-free compounding more easily seen.

Let's say, for example, that in a given year you find that you can make a $2,000 IRA contribution, taking into account the benefit of the tax deduction. You are afraid, however, that you will have to take the money out in a few years to pay tuition bills, or for some other reason.

Here are your choices: if you save through an IRA, you will benefit from the tax deduction now and the tax-free compounding as you go along, but you will pay income tax plus the penalty tax when you withdraw your dollars early. Without the IRA, the situation is reversed. Income taxes will reduce the amount you set aside now and will cut into your annual earnings; but there will be no additional tax to pay when you are ready to withdraw.

Table 8
EFFECTS OF THE PENALTY TAX ON IRA AND NON-IRA INVESTORS

	30% Tax Bracket		50% Tax Bracket	
	With IRA	Without IRA	With IRA	Without IRA
Income available	$2,000	$2,000	$2,000	$2,000
Less: income tax	—	600	—	1,000
Net amount to invest	$2,000	$1,400	$2,000	$1,000
Annual earnings rate	10.0%	10.0%	10.0%	10.0%
Less: income tax	—	3.0	—	5.0
Net earnings rate	10.0%	7.0%	10.0%	5.0%
After 5 years: Value of investment	$3,221	$1,964	$3,221	$1,276
Less: income tax	966	—	1,611	—
Penalty tax	322	—	322	—
Net amount available	$1,933	$1,964	$1,288	$1,276
After 7 years: Value of investment	$3,897	$2,248	$3,897	$1,407
Less: income tax	1,169	—	1,949	—
Penalty tax	390	—	390	—
Net amount available	$2,338	$2,248	$1,558	$1,407

In table 8 I have assumed that you can earn 10 percent on the amount you put aside, inside or outside the IRA. But if it's outside, and you are in the 30 percent tax bracket, your net earnings rate will be cut to 7 percent after taxes; in the 50 percent tax bracket, the net earnings rate will be cut to 5 percent. As the table shows, after five years the IRA tax benefits have completely offset the impact of the penalty tax for an investor in the 50 percent tax bracket, while an IRA investor in the 30 percent bracket is behind by only a few dollars. After seven years, the IRA advantage is unmistakable, especially as the tax bracket increases. If you can earn at a higher rate than 10 percent, the tax savings will offset the penalty more quickly than in the above example. If the rate is less than 10 percent, it will be slower. Using a pocket calculator, you can actually make up your own table for any combination of interest rates and years. (Don't forget that for savings outside the IRA, each year's earnings have to be reduced by the appropriate income tax.)

The 10 percent penalty, as you can see, is really very modest. There is no penalty imposed on the amounts left in your IRA, no curtailment of your future contributions, and no requirement that such *premature distributions,* as they are termed, be on an all-or-none basis. Except for your paying the ordinary income tax and the penalty tax on the amount withdrawn, the rest of your IRA goes on as before. You could hardly ask for a better deal.

There is one small piece of paperwork that is required if you withdraw money from your IRA before age fifty-nine and a half. IRS Form 5329, "Return for Individual Retirement Arrangement Taxes," must be filed together with your IRS Form 1040 if you owe a penalty tax on premature distributions (or on excess contributions or excess accumulations—see appendix C). The form is simple and you shouldn't let it bother you. Check with your tax adviser to make sure there has been no change in the IRS requirements.

In the Introduction, the question was raised, "What if I can't save?," and I pointed out that it is often worth taking money out of an existing savings account (or out of stocks, bonds, or whatever) in order to get the IRA tax advantage. Many people will hesitate to do this because of the fear of "locking up" their money in an IRA. As you can see, the "lock-up" is a rather soft arrangement that shouldn't frighten you. Unless you *know* you will want to take the money out in a year or two, there is no reason to be overly fearful.

There may even be situations where it makes sense to *borrow* to make your IRA contribution—assuming that you have a reasonable prospect of paying the loan back in the future. This type of situation varies so much from case to case that I can't generalize. But note that you can't use any part of your IRA as *security* for a loan. That counts as one of the transactions that are prohibited in an IRA.

By now you have probably figured out for yourself that there may be cases where the penalty tax is even less burdensome than in the examples given above. What if you are in a lower tax bracket when you withdraw money than when you put it in? Let's say that you have $2,000 to spare for your IRA in a year when you are in a 50 percent tax bracket, but that three years later you have financial problems, you have dropped to a 30 percent bracket, and you need to take the money out. (We'll again assume that your IRA earns a 10 percent rate of return, and that you stay in the 50 percent bracket for the first two years, so that your net earnings rate outside the IRA is 5 percent.)

	With IRA	Without IRA
Income available	$2,000	$2,000
Less: Income tax (50%)	—	1,000
Net amount to invest	2,000	1,000
After three years:		
Value of investment	2,662	1,158
Less: Income tax (30%)	779	—
Penalty tax	266	—
Net amount available	$1,597	$1,158

In the example above, your IRA has worked as a highly flexible tax-shelter arrangement, with money going in when your tax bracket is high and coming out when the tax is lower. If your tax bracket is ten percentage points lower when you withdraw, that offsets the penalty tax immediately, and the other benefits are pure gain.

PENALTIES YOU CAN AVOID

If you need to take money out of your IRA before retirement, the penalty tax probably won't be a major problem. But there are other problems that may require a little planning.

Be sure that your investments can be turned into cash without difficulty. Some investments can be sticky. You may have bought bank CDs with a fixed maturity date and the usual "substantial penalty for early withdrawal." Or—and this is potentially much more costly—you may own a common stock fund, or some other investment that fluctuates in price, and find that you need cash just when the market has temporarily gone down.

Obviously, a 15 percent dip in the stock market can be more expensive than a 10 percent penalty tax. For money that may have to be withdrawn from your IRA within a year or two, I suggest that you forego the more exciting growth possibilities and keep the money in a money market fund where the results are predictable.

THE REAL PENALTY

I have spent this chapter telling you how easy it is to withdraw cash from your IRA before retirement. Now I have one final word of advice:

Don't do it.

At least, don't do it unless you have to. The real purpose of an IRA is a valid one: to help you save for old age and retirement. Inflation is a fact of life, the costs of a comfortable retirement continue to climb, and there is a happy probability that you will live substantially longer than your parents or grandparents. So you will need all the retirement income you can get, and your IRA will be an important supplement to other retirement income. It may even be your *main* source of income.

The IRA rules are generous in some respects, but the $2,000 you are allowed to put in annually is not a tremendous amount. *Only by letting this money compound for as many years as possible* will you be able to make the most of your IRA. The real penalty for taking money out of your IRA prematurely is that *there's no way to put the money back in.* You permanently lose the possibility of tax-free compounding on whatever sums are removed. The $1,000 you took out this year, if left in your IRA, might possibly have turned into $10,000 twenty years from now. You can be sure that it will grow much less outside of your IRA.

7

KEEPING YOUR IRA AHEAD OF INFLATION

It takes careful planning to keep ahead of inflation. In the 1970s, inflation took people largely unawares and cut deeply into the value of almost everyone's savings. An intelligent investment program should be designed to prevent this from ever happening again.

The problem presented by inflation is really twofold: (1) how can you plan for the future when you don't know the value of tomorrow's dollar, and (2) why should you save at all? Why not simply spend the money now before it becomes worthless?

Fortunately, there are positive answers to these questions. In your planning for inflation, your IRA has special importance because it gives you a flexibility that your other retirement arrangements may not offer. Your company retirement plan, for example, may not adjust adequately for inflation, and now there are doubts as to whether Social Security benefits will go on being raised to keep pace with inflation as automatically as in the past. (It's also possible that Social Security benefits may be revised in other ways, or made subject to income tax.) In your IRA, however, you have the opportunity to make your own decisions—you can invest in a way that takes inflation into account. So your IRA can be a key element for dealing with inflation in your total financial planning.

THE INVESTMENT CHOICES

Let me briefly review what has been said in earlier chapters about the impact of inflation on different types of investments.

Because inflation has proved so difficult to forecast, I have put extra emphasis on investments that appear likely to protect you regardless of whether the inflation rate gets better or worse. I have pointed out that as long as investors remain keenly aware of inflation, short-term "market" interest rates will probably have to adjust to the inflation rate sufficiently to give investors a positive return in *real* terms. This has generally been true over the long run. It was *not* true during the 1970s, but the evidence seems to show that the long-run relationship has been restored.

So the banks, thrift institutions, and money market funds—which now generally offer you market rates of interest—should be able to keep you ahead of inflation and give you modest growth in the real value of your investment.

A more fundamental way of dealing with inflation, but one that subjects you to short-term price fluctuations and some additional risks, is through investments in common stocks. We explored the rationale of common stock investments in chapter 2. Common stocks represent the ownership of real corporate assets such as factories, machines, land, and natural resources, which will rise in value with inflation. Moreover, common stock prices reflect corporate profits, and corporations have become accustomed to planning for inflation, so that their profits will generally grow with the inflation rate. All of which means that common stocks, besides being a basically valid investment, are a natural long-run inflation hedge.

We have also seen that there are investments that do *not* naturally adjust to inflation, and that may do well or badly depending on the inflation trend. When you buy bonds, as discussed in chapter 3, you are guaranteed a fixed-interest rate return over several years that reflects today's expectations about inflation. Your flow of dollars remains constant for the life of the bond. If inflation turns out as expected, you will earn a moderate "real" return, usually somewhat higher than you would have earned with a bank or money market fund. If inflation is less than expected, your real return will be higher, and if inflation gets worse, your real return will shrink.

On the opposite side, gold stocks can make you feel happy and prosperous when inflation is running high, but they can lag in the doldrums when the economy is stable. And certain investments in land and other natural resources may act much the same way, though to a less pronounced extent.

CHOOSING A STRATEGY: TO FORECAST OR NOT TO FORECAST

As the above discussion suggests, there are two basic types of strategies you can follow in fortifying your investments against inflation.

The first strategy is fairly simple. As I said earlier, most economic experts have done poorly in forecasting inflation and most amateurs have not done any better. The best investment policy for most people will be one that doesn't require making inflation forecasts. You can follow this strategy by concentrating your investments in the banks and money market funds, or in common stocks—or in some combination of these, if you recognize the advantages of common stocks but feel more comfortable keeping part of your money immune from price fluctuations.

If you don't want to be dependent on inflation forecasts, and if part or all of your IRA is invested in common stocks, it's also important that your common stock list be well diversified. For example, you should *not* put 100 percent of your common stock money into natural resource stocks, or into mutual funds that are concentrated in those stocks. They may work out well eventually, but portfolios of that type have often lagged behind the stock market averages for some time during low inflation periods. A portfolio that intentionally excluded natural resource investments would be just as unbalanced. If you are using common stock funds for your IRA, you might consider balancing one fund concentrated in natural resources against one or two others that are more widely diversified.

The second strategy is more complex, since it involves adjusting your investments from time to time according to changes in the inflation outlook. This means higher risks and also possibly higher rewards. It means that you may invest at times in bonds, or in gold stocks and other specific inflation hedges, and it means that you will also make adjustments within your common stock holdings, sometimes stressing the natural resource stocks, while at other times stressing the "interest sensitive" stocks that act best when the inflation rate is low or declining.

If you are intent on following this strategy, a brokerage IRA will probably give you maximum flexibility in the choice of investments. If you can find a broker who gives you capable advice on coping with inflation, all the better. If not, and if you don't feel qualified to make your own judgments as to individual investments, you can accomplish much the same purpose by using mutual funds—common stock funds of various types, gold funds, and bond funds.

Perhaps I should try more pointedly to discourage you from following this second strategy. Certainly there are risks in trying to anticipate inflation correctly where so many experts have failed. But I prefer to leave the decision to you. Markets tend to run to extremes, and the investor who has the fortitude and detachment not to be caught up with the crowd may outguess the markets on inflation, just as on other matters. If you have that ability, or if you know a broker who has it, good luck.

One more note. In adjusting your IRA investments to inflation, remember that your strategy within your IRA should be coordinated with your *total* financial and retirement planning. If your company pension plan fails to adjust adequately to inflation, all the more reason to concentrate your IRA in common stock investments. On the other hand, if your existing retirement plan is fully invested in common stocks, you may want to include other investments in your IRA. Try to look at the total picture.

THE INFLATION BATTLEGROUND

The inflation outlook depends heavily on political decisions not yet made, and I see no way to make an accurate forecast of what the U.S. inflation rate is likely to be over the next several years. But let me state some general reasons why I believe that the inflation problem will be with us for many years to come.

Politicians and journalists like to focus on simple explanations of inflation—the size of the federal budget deficit, or whether the Federal Reserve is being strict enough in controlling the growth of the money supply. Posing the question in this way makes it appear that the problem could be solved by simple acts of Congress and the Federal Reserve.

There is some truth to this approach, but it is certainly not the whole truth. To understand the problem, one must ask *why* federal budget deficits are so persistent, and *why* the money supply is so difficult to control. The real causes of inflation are not simple. Over the years, the U.S. economy has developed patterns in which every sector has grown accustomed to spending more than it earns or produces. The federal government, with its massive deficits, may be the most obvious offender, but it is not the only one. Consumers are encouraged in a hundred different ways to spend now and pay later. Labor unions routinely expect to win wage increases above what can be paid for by increased productivity. Businesses routinely borrow to expand or to buy out their competitors, convinced that they can repay the borrowings with cheaper dollars in the future. And so it goes. When borrowing and spending increase faster than the basic supply of goods and services, inflation has to follow.

The inflation cures applied in recent years have simply not been adequate to the problem. In fact, the only policy applied with any vigor has been for the Federal Reserve to curtail private spending and borrowing by raising interest rates and, in effect, causing a recession. Not surprisingly, many people find this cure as damaging as the disease. Moreover, a recession reduces Treasury tax receipts, and high interest rates make the Treasury spend more on interest payments, so the federal budget deficit rises, and to this extent the cure actually makes the disease worse.

I think there will eventually be serious attempts to solve the structural problems that encourage inflation. But even then, habits that have been built up over a long period will take time to change. For the near future, your financial planning had better assume that inflation will continue—not at the double-digit rates of 1979–80, but at high enough rates so that the problem cannot be ignored.

But watch for changes in the inflation trend. Curiously enough, the IRA itself may be a sign of change. For the first time, the government is giving ordinary individuals a major tax benefit as an incentive to save. Millions of Americans will make an effort to gain from this benefit, and billions of dollars will be saved that would otherwise have been spent.

Will saving become fashionable again? If so, it will mark an important turning point in consumer behavior, and your IRA could be part of a new, and healthier, national economic trend.

8

HOW TO RETIRE RICH

Throughout this book I have stressed that for most people the IRA is a remarkable opportunity to build up savings for the future. But until now, I have carefully avoided giving you specific projections of how your IRA dollars are likely to grow, simply because such figures can too easily be distorted and misused.

Now, however, I think we have laid the groundwork for making projections intelligently and realistically. And I think we are ready to return to the basic questions that were raised in the Introduction—What will your IRA do for you at retirement? Will you really retire rich? Can your IRA make you a millionaire?

By now you know that the answers to these questions will vary widely for different individuals. The results you get from your IRA will depend very much on your own choices and decisions.

Moreover, we should recognize that the questions have a built-in bias of their own. The barrage of advertising and promotion for IRAs has conjured up visions of wealth and fortune in everyone's mind. No matter how favorable the real possibilities are, they may not live up to the advertisements.

The new IRA law, after all, was aimed at the moderate goal of giving people effective help in saving for their retirement and old age. And the law meets that objective. Even a conservatively managed IRA will help your savings grow far more than would otherwise have been possible and will make your retirement far more comfortable than it would otherwise have been.

But if mere comfort does not satisfy you, and you are intent on wealth and luxury, the IRA may be able to help you there, too. You can aim higher in your IRA by managing your money more intently and by choosing investments with higher growth potential, which carry with them risks of loss and of short-term price fluctuations. This approach carries no guarantees, but we will see that the maximum potential of a risk-taking IRA is very high indeed.

So let's look at the figures. While there may be no absolute answers, we should be able to set out the probabilities in a way that will let you make the choices that are right for you.

THE 12 PERCENT MIRAGE

First, though, we need to dispose of all those tables of results in the IRA brochures and newspaper ads that show your money growing like clockwork over thirty or forty years, with a million dollars or more at the end of the rainbow.

Mark Twain once said that there are three kinds of lies—lies, damned lies, and statistics. Think about these advertisements, and you will understand what Twain had in mind.

If you have read the footnotes to the tables, you know that some interest rate, typically 12 percent, has been assumed in making the calculations. But you also know that the sponsor—in most cases a bank, occasionally a mutual fund—is *not* guaranteeing this rate or any other rate. On a 12 percent assumption, there's no denying that the dollar results are impressive. And to sweeten the pie further, many banks have published tables based on an assumed interest rate of 12 percent *compounded daily,* which works out to an annual yield of 12.94 percent and even bigger dollar numbers.

What's wrong with these statistics? Simply that the assumptions have nothing to do with reality. The interest rates paid by banks and money market funds over the long run are likely to average very modestly above the rate of inflation—perhaps by a margin of 2 to 4 percent. These investments won't pay you 12 percent over any long period of time unless the inflation rate averages between 8 and 10 percent. But if the inflation rate does average between 8 and 10 percent, then the million dollars that you accumulate down the road will be worth only a small fraction of that amount *measured in today's money,* and the figures in the table will have lost all practical meaning.

Obviously, unless inflation is taken into account, any other tables of this type will be part of the same pointless mathematical game, in which you accumulate more and more dollars that are worth less and less. Since there's no way to forecast the exact rate of inflation, you may wonder whether all forecasts are worthless.

Fortunately, there's a simple way to get around the problem cleanly and completely. In this chapter we will talk only about *real* rates of return. Note the word *real.* Your real rate of return is the rate by which the compounded growth rate in your IRA *exceeds* the rate of inflation. Real rates of return, or real growth rates, have some predictability. And by using real growth rates in our projections, we will express the amounts you can accumulate in your IRA in today's dollars—in terms of the value of a dollar today and what it can currently purchase, not in the shrunken dollars that will actually be circulating twenty or thirty years from now. We will in effect have cut the inflation rate out of the problem. The figures will let you know your real purchasing power at retirement, no matter what the inflation rate turns out to be, and no matter how many paper dollars you have in your account at that time.

USING THE FIGURES

Table 9 shows the amount you can accumulate in an IRA over any number of years at different rates of return. Let me repeat that we will read the table in terms of *real* rates of return in order to arrive at results expressed in today's dollars. Since we are concerned with real rates, the table realistically shows rates of return ranging all the way from a low 2 percent—which might be your real rate of return with some banks and money funds—up to highs of 10 and 12 percent, which are rates likely to be earned on a real basis only by the most successful risk-taking forms of investment.

Once the rules are established, using the table is simple. First, let's assume that your IRA is invested in a bank or money market fund. As I have said, either of these will in all probability keep you moderately ahead of inflation, perhaps by 2 or 3 percent. If you

Table 9
HOW YOUR IRA DOLLARS CAN GROW
(results of investing $2,000 a year at different growth rates)

Value at End of	2%	3%	4%
1 Year	$ 2,040	$ 2,060	$ 2,080
2 Years	4,121	4,182	4,243
3	6,243	6,367	6,493
4	8,408	8,618	8,833
5	10,616	10,937	11,266
6	12,869	13,325	13,797
7	15,166	15,785	16,428
8	17,509	18,318	19,166
9	19,899	20,928	22,012
10	22,337	23,616	24,973
11	24,824	26,384	28,052
12	27,361	29,236	31,254
13	29,948	32,173	34,584
14	32,587	35,198	38,047
15	35,279	38,314	41,649
16	38,024	41,523	45,395
17	40,825	44,829	49,291
18	43,681	48,234	53,342
19	46,595	51,741	57,556
20	49,567	55,353	61,938
21	52,598	59,074	66,496
22	55,690	62,906	71,236
23	58,844	66,853	76,165
24	62,061	70,919	81,292
25	65,342	75,106	86,623
26	68,689	79,419	92,168
27	72,102	83,862	97,935
28	75,584	88,438	103,933
29	79,136	93,151	110,170
30	82,759	98,005	116,657
35	101,989	124,552	153,197
40	123,220	155,327	197,653

The above figures assume that an investment of $2,000 is made at the beginning of each year. Values are shown as of the end of each year. No adjustment has been made for income taxes that may be payable when funds are withdrawn.

5%	6%	8%	10%	12%
$ 2,100	$ 2,120	$ 2,160	$ 2,200	$ 2,240
4,305	4,367	4,493	4,620	4,749
6,620	6,749	7,012	7,282	7,559
9,051	9,274	9,733	10,210	10,706
11,604	11,951	12,672	13,431	14,230
14,284	14,788	15,846	16,974	18,178
17,098	17,795	19,273	20,872	22,599
20,053	20,983	22,975	25,159	27,551
23,156	24,362	26,973	29,875	33,097
26,414	27,943	31,291	35,062	39,309
29,834	31,740	35,954	40,769	46,266
33,426	35,764	40,991	47,045	54,058
37,197	40,030	46,430	53,950	62,785
41,157	44,552	52,304	61,545	72,559
45,315	49,345	58,649	69,899	83,507
49,681	54,426	65,500	79,089	95,767
54,265	59,811	72,900	89,198	109,499
59,078	65,520	80,893	100,318	124,879
64,132	71,571	89,524	112,550	142,105
69,439	77,985	98,846	126,005	161,397
75,010	84,785	108,914	140,805	183,005
80,861	91,992	119,787	157,086	207,206
87,004	99,631	131,530	174,995	234,310
93,454	107,729	144,212	194,694	264,668
100,227	116,313	157,909	216,364	298,668
107,338	125,412	172,702	240,200	336,748
114,805	135,056	188,678	266,420	379,398
122,645	145,280	205,932	295,262	427,166
130,878	156,116	224,566	326,988	480,665
139,522	167,603	244,692	361,887	540,585
189,673	236,242	372,204	596,254	966,926
253,680	328,095	559,562	973,704	1,718,285

invest $2,000 on January 1 each year, and earn a 3 percent real rate of return, the *real* value of your IRA in today's dollars will grow as shown in the 3 percent column of the table, with the following results:

	Cost	Value
After 1 year	$ 2,000	$ 2,060
10 years	20,000	23,616
20	40,000	55,353
30	60,000	98,005
40	80,000	155,327

At a real return of 3 percent, you obviously have not managed to accumulate $1 million, at least not in today's dollars. But the nest egg you have built up is one that many people might envy; and, as the table shows, you will take out, in real terms, much more than you put in. Moreover, as we will see shortly, there is a possible extra bonus that can lift your results above the figures shown in the table.

It may be worth repeating once more that the banks and the money funds represent essentially conservative investments that should not be expected to do more than keep you *moderately* ahead of inflation. They will keep you immune from price fluctuations and short-term market risks, but at the same time they will not offer you the possibility of greater long-term growth, which you may achieve if you are willing to accept more risks.

So let us next assume that your IRA is invested in common stocks, either through a brokerage IRA or through common stock mutual funds, and let us also assume for the moment that your results are just in line with the stock market averages. In chapter 2, we saw that over long periods the *average* common stock investment has stayed ahead of inflation by a little better than 6 percent. Assuming that this trend holds—and it seems to have prevailed over a remarkably long time—your *real* results, as shown by the 6 percent column in the table, would be as follows:

	Cost	Value
After 1 year	$ 2,000	$ 2,120
10 years	20,000	27,943
20	40,000	77,985
30	60,000	167,603
40	80,000	328,095

Reasonably impressive, I think. But our discussion of common stocks stressed that there is no reason to settle for merely average results—if you are not a superior manager yourself, it's possible to invest your money with someone who is. There are several good common stock funds that have stayed 2 percent ahead of the market averages over long periods, which means 8 percent ahead of inflation. A very few funds have even managed to stay 4 percent ahead of the averages over the long run, or 10 percent ahead of inflation. So the record shows that real returns of this magnitude are achievable on common stock investments. And at these real rates of return, your results would be as follows:

	Cost	Value at 8%	at 10%
After 1 year	$ 2,000	$ 2,160	$ 2,200
10 years	20,000	31,291	35,062
20	40,000	98,846	126,005
30	60,000	244,692	361,887
40	80,000	559,562	973,704

You will notice that as you work with higher rates, the compounding effect accelerates. Each additional 1 percent in return makes a bigger difference in your results, and each additional year also has a magnified effect.

THE POSTRETIREMENT BONUS

I mentioned earlier that the IRA provides you with an extra bonus, and it is one that people often fail to consider.

The tables we have used all show the buildup of your IRA dollars to the point where you stop contributing and begin to take withdrawals. This may be at age fifty-nine and a half, or sixty-five, or seventy and a half, or somewhere in between. But note that if you take out your money in *installments* rather than in a lump sum, the amount remaining in the IRA *continues to compound tax-free* until the account has all been paid out to you. The higher the real earnings rate, the more this can add to your ultimate payout.

Let's say that you have reached age sixty-five, that you have contributed $2,000 a year to your IRA for thirty years, and that now you have decided to take your money out in equal installments over fifteen years, meanwhile leaving the balance working in the IRA in the same types of investments, and at the same real growth rate, as before. At the real rates of return that we have surveyed, and applying a standard formula, here is how your lump-sum accumulation would translate into a fifteen-year payout:

	3%	6%	8%	10%
Sum at age 65	$ 98,005	$167,603	$244,692	$361,887
Payments per year for 15 years	8,210	17,257	28,587	47,579
Total paid out	123,150	258,855	428,805	713,685

Note that these figures reflect a thirty-year accumulation—say from age thirty-five to sixty-five. If you want to assume a forty-year buildup, for example, from age twenty-five to sixty-five, the results of course will be magnified. The investor who averaged a real return of 8 percent over forty years, and built up a lump sum of $559,000, would actually receive *$980,000* if he or she chose a fifteen-year payout. And the investor who managed to build up to $973,000 at a 10 percent rate of return would take out *$1,920,000* over those same fifteen years.

So there you have over a million dollars from an IRA based on a 10 percent real return—and a few investment managers have actually achieved real returns of more than 10 percent for extended periods.

But I again stress that these maximum returns are not the main point; the main point is that even at more moderate rates of return, the IRA is an opportunity you cannot afford to miss.

Consider, in this regard, what the IRA payout really has cost you. You have put in $2,000 a year, in our examples, but you have taken a tax deduction on the contribution. If you were in the 50 percent tax bracket, the net cost of the contribution to you was only $1,000 a year; if you were in the 25 percent bracket, your net cost was $1,500. Over thirty years, your total net cost on these assumptions might have been $30,000 or $45,000. You will owe income taxes on your withdrawal payments at retirement, but your real net proceeds will still be remarkably higher than your real net cost.

Incidentally, I have used a fifteen-year payout in some of the above installment examples as a realistic schedule under the IRA rules. At age seventy and a half, when you must begin making withdrawals at a certain minimum rate based on life expectancy, the IRS calculates your life expectancy at twelve years for a male and fifteen years for a female (based on 1981 IRS schedules). But this means that if you start the withdrawals five years earlier, at age sixty-five, you can legally stretch the payments over as many as seventeen years (male) or twenty years (female), to age eighty-two or eighty-five, respectively. The payout period can be even longer if it is based on the joint life expectancy of both spouses.

SMALL CAN BE BEAUTIFUL

So far, for simplicity and uniformity, all the examples of IRA results have been put in terms of the $2,000-a-year investor. But realistically, the majority of Americans eligible for an IRA will not be able to set aside that much for an IRA, no matter how well they recognize the advantages. Is there a point to putting aside less?

There certainly is. The rate at which your money grows will be just as favorable for smaller amounts, and the IRA is a great bargain at any level. You can translate all the results in the tables into terms of $1,000 a year simply by dividing by two, or into terms of $500 a year by dividing by four. Given sufficient years, the totals are still impressive.

If you want to calculate the results at some different contribution level, and have forgotten your elementary algebra, simply take out a calculator, refer to the table, and: (1) find the dollar result in the table for the real rate of return and number of years you are assuming; (2) divide that figure by $2,000; and (3) multiply by your expected annual contribution. Result: your buildup in today's dollars.

I still urge you to contribute as much to your IRA as you possibly can. But I also urge you to start an IRA even if you can only contribute very little. At $250 a year, with an 8 percent real growth rate, you could accumulate $30,586 in thirty years, or $69,945 in forty years. Not a fortune, surely, but enough to give you payments of $3,573 or $8,171 a year for fifteen years. Is that worth $250 a year now? I think it is.

PAPER DOLLARS

Earlier in this chapter I said that we would deal only with real rates of return and real accumulations. We have followed that approach consistently. But let's take a brief detour away from real dollars and deal for a moment with paper dollars.

Table 10
HOW INFLATION WILL SHRINK THE DOLLAR

No. of Years	Assumed Annual Inflation Rate							
	3%	4%	5%	6%	8%	10%	12%	14%
0	$1.00	$1.00	$1.00	$1.00	$1.00	$1.00	$1.00	$1.00
5	.86	.82	.78	.75	.68	.62	.57	.52
10	.74	.68	.61	.56	.46	.39	.32	.27
15	.64	.56	.48	.42	.32	.24	.18	.14
20	.55	.46	.38	.31	.21	.15	.10	.07
25	.48	.38	.30	.23	.15	.09	.06	.04
30	.41	.31	.23	.17	.10	.06	.03	.02
35	.36	.25	.18	.13	.07	.04	.02	.01
40	.31	.21	.14	.10	.05	.02	.01	.005

Look at table 10. It shows the value of the dollar in the future at various inflation rates, in terms of purchasing power measured in today's dollars. The table is simple enough. For example, after thirty years at an average inflation rate of 3 percent, the dollar will be worth forty-one cents in today's purchasing power. At 6 percent inflation, it would be worth seventeen cents. And so on for different inflation rates and different numbers of years.

To go from today's dollars to those depreciated dollars, simply divide by the factor in the table. For example, in table 9 we have the example of an IRA with a 10 percent growth rate, accumulating $361,887 in thirty years. That was in real terms—in today's dollars. If you assume a 6 percent inflation rate, the investor's current dollars at that time would actually be $361,887 divided by .17, or approximately $2,130,000. Experiment a little with the figures, and you will see that becoming a millionaire on paper probably won't be difficult at all. But if you want to know what your money really will be worth—stick to today's dollars.

FOR MAXIMUM RESULTS

Throughout this book I have stressed the great potential of tax-free compounding. At the risk of boring you, let me make the point again. Many people think of the IRA tax advantage only in terms of the immediate tax deduction. These people will make the mistake of reducing or eliminating their contributions in years when their tax bracket is low, or failing to contribute in the early years when they should be beginning to build up a tax-sheltered pool of money in their IRA. Following the same logic (or lack of it), they may be careless about managing their IRA investments.

Don't fall into that trap. If you want maximum results from your IRA, you need to get every possible dollar working within the tax shelter. For example, an individual who starts an IRA at age thirty, puts in $2,000 a year, and invests at a 6 percent growth rate will accumulate $236,242 by age sixty-five. Prior to age thirty, his income may have been low, or he may not have thought that the IRA contributions were important. But if he had started an IRA five years earlier, at age twenty-five, and managed to put in $10,000 more, he would have ended up at age sixty-five with $328,095—a difference of $91,853, all due to that original $10,000.

The figures we have looked at above have probably suggested some other lessons to you. First, we have seen that a variation of only 1 percent in the rate of return can make a surprising difference in your total results over thirty or forty years. So if additional care and effort on your part can produce an additional 1 percent return, the effort will be well worth it.

Of course, differences in return will depend primarily on the degree of risk and uncertainty you are willing to assume. I don't want to urge you to take more risks than you can feel comfortable with in your choice of investments. But you have seen that the possible rewards in terms of higher return can be very impressive over the years. If you are the type of investor who has never ventured beyond a bank or a money market fund, you owe it to yourself to take some time to consider the alternatives, particularly the common stock mutual funds.

A less important difference, but one still worth considering, is the difference between making your contribution early or late in the year. All of the above examples have assumed that your total IRA contribution for the year is made at the earliest possible date, on January 1. I'm well aware that many people will make their contributions later in the year, or even close to the following April 15. But the advantage of a January 1 contribution, over the years, may be greater than you think. The specific advantage will depend on your contribution level and your rate of return, but here's a typical example. We saw that an investment of $2,000 each January 1 at a real return of 8 percent would produce a buildup of $244,692 in today's dollars at the end of thirty years. If the investor had waited until December 31 each year to make his contribution, his ending total would have been reduced to $226,566; if his contribution for each year had been made on the following April 15, his total would have been cut further, to $221,700.

IRA VERSUS NON-IRA

A final point about the IRA double tax advantage: Wouldn't a consistent savings program do nearly as well without it? No, it wouldn't. The differences are striking, especially in the higher tax brackets. Without the tax deduction, you would have less to invest each year; without tax-free compounding, income taxes would cut into each year's earnings and cause your money to compound at a lower growth rate. We have seen that a small difference in the compounding rate can make a great difference in total results over the years. Even though you will eventually pay income taxes on your withdrawals, the IRA advantage is dramatic.

In chapter 6, we saw that in five years, the IRA advantage was sufficient to offset the 10 percent penalty tax on early withdrawals. Going further, table 11 compares an IRA and a non-IRA savings program over thirty years, assuming a real earnings rate of 8 percent annually for each. I have tried to give the IRA investor the least possible advantage by assuming, somewhat unrealistically, that he or she is in as high a tax bracket at retirement as during the accumulation years, and that the IRA is withdrawn in a lump sum, with full income taxes immediately deducted. The non-IRA saver, of course, has paid taxes every year and has no tax to pay at the end. The score, assuming a 50 percent tax bracket for each: $122,346 net after tax for the IRA investor, $58,328 for the non-IRA investor. Assuming a low 25 percent tax bracket, the advantage is reduced, but the IRA investor would still be ahead by $183,519 to $125,702. If you like playing with figures, you can use table 9 to work out further examples; simply remember that for the non-IRA investor, income taxes reduce not only the initial savings but also the compound growth rate.

Table 11
COMPARISON OF AN IRA AND A NON-IRA
SAVINGS PROGRAM
(30-Year Period)

| | 50% Tax Bracket | | 25% Tax Bracket | |
	With IRA	Without IRA	With IRA	Without IRA
Income Available	$ 2,000	$ 2,000	$ 2,000	$ 2,000
Less: Current Income Tax	—	1,000	—	500
Net Amount to Invest	$ 2,000	$ 1,000	$ 2,000	$ 1,500
Annual Earnings Rate	8.0%	8.0%	8.0%	8.0%
Less: Current Income Tax	—	4.0	—	2.0
Net Annual Earnings Rate	8.0%	4.0%	8.0%	6.0%
Value of Account after 30 Years	$244,692	$58,328	$244,692	$125,702
Less: Income Tax	122,346	—	61,173	—
Net Amount	$122,346	$58,328	$183,519	$125,702

A CRITICAL ASSUMPTION

Now that we have looked at the IRA tax advantage from every aspect I can think of, I must admit that there is one critical assumption that we have not discussed.

Because inflation will erode the value of a dollar, we have carefully used the tables to show results in *real* terms—in today's dollars. But what about the $2,000 annual contributions? There's no doubt that because of inflation, $2,000 in paper dollars will be worth less and less as the years go by. But if your contributions don't hold steady in *real* terms, all the results we have been discussing will shrink far below what we have projected.

The critical assumption is that Congress *will continue to raise the IRA contribution limits* periodically in dollar terms, so that over the years, your average contribution will be equivalent to at least $2,000 annually in today's dollars.

This assumption can't be proved, but there are several reasons why it makes good sense. First, Congress regularly reexamines the tax rules, and adjusts various limitations for inflation. In 1982, for example, when the new tax law extended the IRA to all wage earners, it also raised the contribution limit from $1,500 to $2,000 and, in the case of spousal IRAs, from $1,750 to $2,250.

Second, there's a particularly encouraging precedent. When Keogh retirement plans for self-employed persons were first introduced in 1963, the maximum allowable tax deduction was $1,250. Over the next few years, this was raised to $7,500. In 1982 the limit was boosted to $15,000, and legislation was passed to raise it to $30,000 in 1984. This example suggests the possibility that the IRA limits may be raised over the years, not only in dollar terms but also in real terms. In that case, the ultimate real potential of your IRA could be much higher than we have projected.

Third, the millions of new IRA planholders will make up a large group of voters whom Congress will not easily be able to ignore. Because of the great number of people who will have a stake in the IRA program, there will be continual pressure to make the program more generous rather than less. True, the IRA tax deduction will cut into government tax revenues to some measurable extent. But if the new law successfully adds to the nation's savings, while benefiting millions of wage and salary earners at a wide range of income levels, it will not be an easy program to tamper with politically. The odds are that the IRA is here to stay and very likely on a bigger scale as time goes along.

RARE CREATION, RARE OPPORTUNITY

I began this book by saying that the IRA is that rarest of creations— a government tax program that actually helps you. In a financial world that seems to grow increasingly more difficult and complex, the IRA is a simple innovation that is likely to yield a remarkable range of benefits. It helps individuals to save for retirement; it gives them a powerful tool for planning their own financial futures; it rewards individual saving, rather than spending; and on the larger scale, as mentioned above, it appears certain to add to the flow of the nation's savings.

The IRA tax shelter gives you a strong assist to your own long-term savings program. Yet, if the need arises, you will be able to tap these tax-sheltered savings with only a modest penalty. You may have found reason in the past to be suspicious of new laws, new programs, and new promises, especially where your money is concerned. In this case, you can drop your suspicions. The government has given you a tax shelter—take advantage of it.

But taking advantage means more than opening your IRA and making annual contributions. As we have seen, it means *managing* your IRA for best results. Whether you decide on a conservative IRA, a risk-taking IRA, or some balance between the two, take the time to watch your IRA carefully and to make the best possible choices within the framework you have chosen. Will you make a million? Not necessarily. But the potential is there. With patience, care, and alertness, your IRA should reward your efforts and pay off handsomely.

APPENDIXES

APPENDIX A

IRAS AND KEOGHS FOR THE SELF-EMPLOYED

If you were self-employed before 1982, you had to choose between a Keogh retirement plan and an IRA. Now, you can have both. "Self-employed" includes all fully self-employed professionals, sole proprietors, independent contractors, and members of partnerships, with or without employees. It also includes anyone who has part-time earnings from self-employment.

It is worth noting that effective in 1982, the maximum annual dollar contribution to Keogh plans—also known as self-employed retirement plans or HR-10 plans—was raised from $7,500 to $15,000. (The percentage ceiling remained at 15 percent of earned income.) So, in 1982 and 1983, if your self-employed income is $100,000 or above, you can make tax-deductible contributions of up to $17,000 annually for your retirement—$15,000 to your Keogh plan and $2,000 to your IRA.

If your spouse has no earned income and is eligible for a spousal IRA, the total possible contribution is $17,250 ($15,000 plus $2,250). But in that case consider another possibility. If your spouse can be employed legitimately in your business or profession, he or she can then have an independent IRA, opening the way to an additional tax deduction of up to $2,000. The same reasoning applies to any other family members who can legitimately be put on the payroll.

The new tax law passed in September 1982 will have far-reaching effects on Keogh plans. It provides that taking effect generally in 1984, most of the differences between Keogh and corporate retirement plans will be eliminated, with uniform rules that will greatly increase the flexibility of Keogh plans and the benefits available. For the simplest types of Keogh plans, the percentage limit on contributions will be increased and the maximum dollar limitation will be raised to $30,000 (with cost-of-living increases in this maximum in subsequent years, starting in 1986).

Obviously, if you are self-employed and in a high income bracket, your tax and retirement benefits will come primarily from your Keogh plan. But if your earnings are $13,333 or below, the 15 percent you can contribute to a Keogh plan for 1982 will be less than the flat $2,000 you can contribute to an IRA.

(The Keogh percentage limit is suspended for certain persons at the lower end of the income range. In 1982, the maximum Keogh contribution for self-employed persons with earned income of $750 to $5,000 is a flat $750, and those with self-employed earned income below $750 can contribute part or all of this earned income. But note that this concession is not available to anyone whose adjusted gross income *from all sources* is over $15,000.)

Note that if you are self-employed part-time, you may very well have three retirement plans: your employer's plan, your own Keogh plan, and your IRA. Note also, however, that no matter how many different jobs or occupations you may have, you are only entitled to a *single IRA deduction* of up to $2,000 annually (or $2,250 with a spousal IRA). Instead of contributing to a separate IRA, you can make additional voluntary tax-deductible contributions of up to $2,000 a year to your Keogh plan, if the plan is worded to permit this option. These contributions follow basically the same rules as IRA contributions, and have generally the same tax advantages.

I will assume that if you are self-employed, you are already familiar with the basic provisions of Keogh plans. In some respects the workings of Keogh plans and IRAs are similar, and many of the sponsors of IRAs also offer IRS-approved Keogh plans. However, it may be useful to review very briefly a few of the major differences between Keogh plans and IRAs.

EMPLOYEES

A Keogh plan for a self-employed person (or partnership) must generally also cover employees. The IRA is for an individual alone and is not affected in any way by employees. (Any Keogh planholder with employees should consult an attorney or tax adviser to make sure that the rules are being followed, and to adjust the plan for the provisions of the new law that become effective in 1984.)

TAXABILITY OF DISTRIBUTIONS

All distributions from an IRA are taxed basically as ordinary income, even in the case of lump-sum distributions. But a lump-sum distribution from a Keogh plan is generally eligible for the special tax treatment accorded to lump-sum distributions from qualified plans. These special provisions are so favorable that they should be studied by anyone who is preparing to take distributions from a Keogh plan, or who is contemplating a rollover of a lump-sum distribution from a Keogh plan into an IRA. Consult your tax adviser and ask your local IRS office for Publication 575, *Pension and Annuity Income*.

VOLUNTARY CONTRIBUTIONS

If a Keogh plan includes employees, all participants are permitted to make additional voluntary *nondeductible* contributions to the plan of up to 10 percent of compensation under certain rules. For sole proprietors, and for partners with more than a 10 percent interest in the capital or profits of the partnership, there is also a flat dollar limit of $2,500 annually. While these contributions are not tax-deductible, once in the plan, they benefit from the advantage of earning and compounding tax-free. These voluntary nondeductible payments to a Keogh plan should not be confused with the voluntary *deductible* contributions mentioned above and in appendix B, which take the place of contributions to a separate IRA. The tax law does not permit additional nondeductible contributions to IRAs.

OPENING DATE

In an IRA, contributions for a given year may be made up to the date when the tax return for that year is due (including extensions), and the IRA also may be *opened* at any time up until that date. In a Keogh plan, the same time limit applies to contributions, but the plan must be *adopted* (i.e., opened and in existence) by the last day of the tax year—that is, by December 31 for persons on a calendar-year basis.

Keogh planholders who are interested in more information should obtain and read IRS Publication 560, *Tax Information on Self-Employed Retirement Plans*. Before leaving the subject of Keogh plans, I will make two obvious points. First, when deciding on investments for your Keogh plan, the same principles apply that have been set forth in this book for IRAs. Second, if your IRA and Keogh plan are set up as two separate accounts, coordinate the investments—plan them as a unit.

If you are a self-employed person with high income, the changes in the Keogh contribution limits mean that you will now be able to provide handsomely for your retirement. In chapter 8, we examined the real prospects of building up capital for retirement in an IRA, with contributions limited to $2,000 a year. Obviously, if you can set aside $17,000 a year tax-free ($32,000 a year beginning in 1984), the possibilities are enormous.

APPENDIX B

EMPLOYER IRA PROGRAMS

What if your employer offers a ready-made IRA program?

As the new IRA law went into effect, a remarkable number of major companies began to offer their employees IRAs through payroll deductions. These payroll-deduction IRAs are no different from any other IRA. Instead of you putting in the money directly, your employer makes regular deductions from your pay and sends the money to your IRA sponsor. It's as simple as that.

Note that in this type of arrangement, your employer is *not* contributing to your IRA. He is simply making *your* contribution convenient and automatic. He will probably pick up the costs of administering the payroll deduction procedure. He will probably *not* pick up the cost of the regular IRA account fees charged by the plan sponsor and/or custodian, but he may save you money by negotiating a lower fee than you would obtain otherwise.

Whether the employer has made the arrangements with a bank, an insurance company, or a mutual fund group, you are likely to be offered more than one investment alternative. The mutual fund groups have made a strong bid for this type of business, based on their ability to offer the employee a wide range of investment choices under one roof, with simple arrangements for switching from one to another. But even if the sponsor is a bank or insurance company, you should be offered a choice between a fixed-income investment and an equity (common stock) program.

The details of the mutual fund plans vary widely. Some plans permit you to contribute as little as $20 per month, while others have higher requirements. If you want your investment divided among two or more of the funds in a fund group, you will probably have to meet the minimum requirement for each fund separately. There may also be a minimum requirement—perhaps $500 or $1,000—on the amount that can be moved from one fund to another. The fund group will ordinarily send you quarterly statements of your account, showing the contributions made during the period, any dividends reinvested, and the balance in the account at the close. The account is basically your own, and you can make your own direct additional contributions to supplement the payroll deduction amounts, as long as the aggregate doesn't exceed the $2,000 annual limit.

The fees that may be deducted from your account vary greatly from sponsor to sponsor. A few sponsors, eager to get this type of group business, are offering corporate IRA plans with no fees at all to the employee. Others are charging higher fees on corporate IRAs than on regular IRAs, in order to offset the high cost of servicing a large number of small accounts making frequent small payments.

This variety of fees means that you should pay careful attention to the fee structure. If, as an employee, you are putting $2,000 a year into your IRA, a fee of $10 or $12 per year will not make a large difference. But if you expect to contribute only $500 or $600, such a fee will in effect cut 2 percent off your annual contribution. In that case, you will have extra reason to compare the payroll-deduction IRA with the alternatives that are open to you if you start your own IRA independently.

Why are employers taking the trouble to offer these plans? Many employers believe that the payroll-deduction plans are a convenience that employees will expect and appreciate; they hope the plans will encourage employee loyalty. Many employers also believe in the goals of the IRA program and genuinely want to encourage the greatest possible participation by employees.

What are the advantages for the employee? There's no denying the convenience of payroll deductions and, if you can afford to contribute only a very small amount to an IRA, the payroll-deduction arrangement may permit smaller regular payments than many sponsors would otherwise accept.

But ultimately, as I have stressed throughout this book, the test of an IRA has to be its investments. If the investments available through an employer IRA are equal to those you would choose for yourself, there's no great harm in the convenience of payroll deductions. (I would rather see you make your total IRA contribution in January, so that the money can earn interest or dividends tax-free for you throughout the whole year; but I recognize that for many people this may not be practical.) If the investments are not what you would choose, then forego the convenience of the payroll-deduction arrangement and go shopping for your own IRA.

There's no easy way to generalize about the quality of investments that you will be offered in a payroll-deduction IRA. Your employer has probably puzzled over the selection process. Technically, he is simply making certain investments *available* through payroll deductions, and is *not* recommending them; he doesn't want that legal responsibility, but neither does he want a group of disgruntled employees. You can be reasonably sure that considerable thought has gone into the choice of investments to be made available by your employer.

However, because of practical limitations, the employer can offer only a limited number of investment choices. He will probably narrow the choice to a single sponsor offering a certain range of investments. He may choose a sponsor based on a superior investment record, but he may also make a choice based on low fees, or administrative services, or other considerations. From your point of view, looking twenty or thirty years down the road, the choice of investments is far more important than anything else.

AN IRA ALTERNATIVE

There's another type of arrangement that some employers will offer as a way of giving employees the advantages of an IRA. The law permits an employer to amend his regular qualified retirement plan so that it can accept "voluntary deductible contributions" from employees. In this case, you make your contribution of up to

$2,000 annually directly to your employer's plan, but take the tax deduction as if you had contributed to a regular IRA.

Because this type of arrangement creates certain administrative headaches for the employer, it may not be widely offered. However, if your company should make this option available, there may be certain income tax and estate tax advantages that you should explore. Your employer's plan may be drawn up in such a way that you can defer your withdrawal payments to a later age than in a regular IRA, and there may also be some deferral of the income taxes payable. Check with your employer or tax adviser on the details. The real test of this type of plan, like any other, must be the quality of the investment choices.

OTHER EMPLOYER OPTIONS

The deductible voluntary contributions are a substitute for opening your own IRA. There are certain other types of employer plans that are *not* IRA substitutes, technically speaking, but that may have a special relationship to your IRA. Here are a few of the employer-sponsored savings and retirement plans that deserve mention:

Simplified Employee Pension The Simplified Employee Pension, or SEP-IRA for short, is technically a special form of IRA. It is, as the name implies, a simplified employer-sponsored plan, distinct and different from your own IRA. Your employer's contributions to the SEP-IRA may be up to 15 percent of your compensation or $15,000, whichever is less (these limits are scheduled to be increased in 1984), and contributions may be made beyond age seventy and a half if you are still employed. If your employer establishes a SEP-IRA, he should permit you to set up your SEP-IRA account with a sponsor of your choice; but not all IRA sponsors have gone through the extra legal steps required for them also to offer SEP-IRAs.

If your employer establishes a SEP-IRA, *you can still have your own separate IRA* and contribute up to $2,000 a year, just as if your employer maintained a regular pension or profit-sharing plan. Or, rather than start a separate IRA, you can make your own contribution of up to $2,000 directly to the SEP-IRA (in addition to your employer's contribution), and still take the tax deduction.

Salary Reduction Plans Some employers offer plans under which you voluntarily elect to have your salary reduced, with the difference then contributed to a savings plan where the money accumulates for your benefit tax-free. You do not pay income taxes on the amount contributed, so that the contribution resembles an IRA contribution from an income tax point of view. But the salary reduction plan has additional advantages:

1. Permitted contributions may be greater than in an IRA.

2. The amount contributed is not subject to Social Security taxes.

3. Penalties on early withdrawals are likely to be less burdensome.

4. At retirement, unlike the case with an IRA, you are permitted to take advantage of the special income tax treatment applicable to lump-sum distributions from qualified retirement plans.

5. In some plans, the employer matches your own contributions to the plan according to some fixed percentage.

Nothing prevents you legally from having an IRA *in addition to* your employer's salary-reduction plan. But if you can't afford to set aside dollars for both plans, ask your employer to help you compare the benefits. An important point to consider is whether the investment choices in the salary-reduction plan meet your standards. If they do, the salary-reduction plan may be the winner of the comparison, particularly if you will receive matching contributions from your employer to help you build up your account.

Other Savings Plans You may also be offered the type of savings plan in which your contributions are made from after-tax income, with no reduction in income taxes. This is obviously less attractive, but it may still bear comparison with an IRA if you can only afford one or the other. If your employer matches your contributions to the plan on a generous percentage basis, the savings plan may still give you more benefits than an IRA, especially if you are in a low tax bracket and derive only limited benefit from the IRA tax deduction.

APPENDIX C

ADDITIONAL IRA RULES

The Introduction to this book set down the most basic rules about IRAs. Here you will find answers to some additional questions about how your IRA works—what you can and can't do, and how the tax benefits apply.

I want to focus on the main points, and not include every detailed regulation that may apply to your IRA. If you wish to become expert on the details, the best source is Internal Revenue Service (IRS) Publication 590, *Tax Information on Individual Retirement Arrangements*, available through your local IRS office. This consists of about ten pages of tightly packed fine print, and covers both the rules that are applicable to everyone and an array of special cases. Surprisingly, it's quite readable. And it's free.

Note that in special cases, particularly when you deal with such problems as divorce or death, it is a mistake for you to try to act as your own lawyer or accountant. In such cases, get professional advice. Remember that as your IRA grows, the total dollar amounts involved will be substantial, and mistakes are likely to be expensive.

You should talk to a lawyer about the designation of beneficiary under your IRA, to make sure that it coordinates with your other estate planning. When you are ready to begin taking withdrawals from your IRA, it is wise to discuss the withdrawal schedule with your tax adviser. And if you are considering a rollover from a qualified pension or profit-sharing plan into a special rollover IRA (see below), you should certainly consult your tax adviser about the consequences and alternatives. Laws and regulations in the retirement plan area have been changing rapidly, and no book can take the place of good professional advice.

Subject to that warning, I hope that the following information will prove useful.

CONTRIBUTIONS

Can I carry over an unused deduction to a subsequent year?

It is worth repeating: if you don't take advantage of the full IRA deduction in a given year, it *cannot* be carried forward. So while the law gives you complete flexibility in varying your contributions within the limit, or omitting contributions entirely in a given year, it is worth making every effort to make the maximum $2,000 contribution (or $2,250 in the case of a spousal IRA) each year.

What happens in case of divorce?

An IRA can figure as an asset in a marital settlement, and you should ask your lawyer for advice as to the tax consequences of any proposed disposition. In one of the more esoteric provisions of the IRA rules, a divorced person for whom a spousal IRA was established at least five years before the divorce may be able to contribute to the IRA based on alimony rather than on earned income. But the maximum contribution under this provision is $1,125, and so it is only useful if earned income is less than $1,125.

Can I contribute securities to my IRA?

No. Except in the case of a special rollover IRA (see below), contributions must be in cash. If you were hoping to avoid the capital gains tax on securities by contributing them to your IRA, the rules don't permit it.

DISTRIBUTIONS

When can distributions begin?

Withdrawals from your IRA can begin without penalty when

you reach age fifty-nine and a half, and can be made at your discretion from that age to age seventy and a half. You *must* start receiving distributions before the end of the year in which you reach age seventy and a half, and the distributions must be a minimum amount per year based on your life expectancy, or the joint life expectancy of you and your spouse. For example, if you are a single woman aged seventy and a half, the IRS figures your life expectancy to be fifteen years. If you have accumulated $300,000 in your IRA, the minimum amount that must be distributed to you in the first year is $300,000 divided by fifteen, or $20,000.

How are distributions taxed?

All amounts withdrawn after age fifty-nine and a half are taxed as ordinary income in the year withdrawn. If you take periodic payments, you are taxed each year only on the amount actually paid out to you. If you purchase a lifetime annuity, you are also taxed only on the amounts as actually received. If you take the money in a lump sum, you do *not* benefit from the special treatment that applies to lump-sum distributions from qualified employer plans, but, as in any case when your income rises sharply, you may benefit from the regular five-year income averaging provisions of the tax law. If you are age sixty-five or older, the withdrawals are ordinary income that should be taken into account in calculating any possible retirement income credit.

The new tax law passed in 1982 imposes income tax withholding on all retirement plan distributions (including IRAs) beginning January 1, 1983. But the recipient can make a simple election *not* to have taxes withheld and your IRA sponsor or custodian is required to notify you of this option.

What if I take money out before age fifty-nine and a half?

As stated in chapter 6, you pay a penalty tax of 10 percent of the amount withdrawn, in addition to ordinary income tax. However, if you become permanently disabled, you may withdraw amounts before that age without penalty.

What other penalties must I be concerned with?

There is a moderate penalty tax on excess contributions over the permitted limit, unless the excess is withdrawn from your IRA before the due date for filing your tax return. (However, Congress

107

has been asked to consider legislation that would permit additional contributions on a nondeductible basis, which would allow more money to compound tax-free within your IRA.) There is a stiff penalty tax if you fail to withdraw money after age seventy and a half at the required rate; however, the IRS may suspend the penalty if you can show that you are taking steps promptly to correct the error. And there are certain "prohibited transactions" that may cause your whole IRA to lose its tax-exempt status, in which case the whole value of the IRA becomes taxable to you immediately as ordinary income—and if you are under age fifty-nine and a half, you are subject to the 10 percent penalty tax in addition to ordinary income tax.

What are these prohibited transactions?

You may not sell property to your IRA, or receive "unreasonable compensation" for managing it. You may not borrow money from your IRA. If you use any part of your IRA as *security* for a loan, the part of the account so pledged is treated as a distribution and is included in your gross income—subject to income tax and also, if you are under age fifty-nine and a half, to the penalty tax.

I thought you said that I could borrow money in order to make a regular contribution to my IRA.

The rules on borrowing may be confusing. You can certainly borrow to make contributions to your IRA, as long as you do not *pledge* any part of the IRA as collateral for the loan. However, you may not borrow money *from* your IRA. In addition, the IRA account may not borrow in order to make investments—note the prohibition mentioned in chapter 4 against buying securities on margin.

What about the ban on investing in gold or jewels?

Beginning in 1982, you are not permitted to buy "collectibles" for your IRA. This includes works of art, metals (including gold), gems, stamps or coins, rugs or antiques, etc. Any money applied to purchase such a collectible would be treated as a premature distribution. (You can, however, buy gold mining stocks. See chapter 3.)

What happens to my IRA if I die?

If you die before the amounts in your IRA are fully withdrawn, the balance is payable to your beneficiary or beneficiaries according to various options. For each IRA in which you invest, you should file a designation of beneficiary with the sponsor, and it is strongly advisable to consult with your attorney when making this designation. Similarly, an attorney or tax adviser should be consulted in choosing distribution options for a beneficiary, especially since the law has been changing in this area. There is no penalty tax payable by a beneficiary if you die before age fifty-nine and a half.

What taxes do my beneficiaries pay?

The general rule applies, that all amounts withdrawn from your IRA are taxable to a beneficiary as ordinary income in the year received. For a planholder dying before 1983, federal *estate* tax can be avoided completely by arranging for payment to be made to a beneficiary in substantially equal installments extending for at least three years after the planholder's death; however, the new tax law approved in 1982 provides that for a planholder dying after December 31, 1982, no more than $100,000 can be excluded from estate tax in this fashion.

What taxes do I pay when I switch my IRA investments?

No tax at all. As we saw in chapter 5, there is no capital gains tax on gains in an IRA. A transfer of IRA assets from one custodian to another may occasionally involve small processing fees, but there is no tax. Even if the money is paid out to you temporarily and technically creates a rollover, this is a nontaxable event—the distribution is not taxable to you, and you of course get no tax deduction when you put the money back into a new IRA account within sixty days.

What about a special rollover that is not from another IRA?

If you receive a lump-sum distribution from an employer's qualified plan, you may roll over the distribution (in whole or in part) tax-free to an IRA if the rollover is executed within sixty days after the distribution is completed. Any amounts you contributed to your employer's plan are excluded from the rollover. A lump-sum distribution (defined as distribution of your complete share in your employer's plan within a calendar year) is common when someone retires, or leaves an employer, or when an employer's plan is discontinued. However, before rolling over such a distribution into an IRA, you should consult a tax adviser, since there are special tax benefits available when a lump-sum distribution is taken in cash that are not available on distributions from an IRA.

If I do set up a special rollover IRA, do I then make my regular IRA contributions to the same account?

No, the rules make it advisable to maintain two separate accounts, and to make your annual tax-deductible contributions into a separate regular IRA account. The special rollover account carries certain special advantages (particularly the ability to roll the account over once again into an employer's qualified plan), which are lost if regular annual contributions are intermingled with the rollover account.

What reports do I file with the IRS?

Ordinarily, you are not required to file any special form with the IRS. Form 1040 already has a simple line for taking your IRA deduction, and the IRS has indicated that Form 1040A (the short form) will have the same. However, you are required to file Form 5329 if you owe any of the IRA penalty taxes—the tax on excess contributions, the tax on premature distributions before age fifty-nine and a half, and the tax on "excess accumulations," i.e., underdistributions after age seventy and a half. And since IRS regulations may change, you should periodically review the requirements with your tax adviser.

What is an IRA disclosure statement?

The rules require that any IRA sponsor must give you a disclosure statement when you set up an IRA. The disclosure statement must include certain general information about IRAs, and must provide specifics about the sponsor's particular plan, including all fees and charges. You have the right to cancel your IRA and receive a full refund during the first seven days after you receive the sponsor's disclosure statement. Some sponsors give you the disclosure statement when your IRA is set up and allow you seven days in which to cancel; others provide you with a disclosure statement in advance and will take your order only after the seven-day period is up. Be careful—some IRA purchase applications require you to affirm that you have received the disclosure statement seven days prior to the purchase, whether you actually have received it that early or not. When you sign the application, you may be limiting your right to cancellation and refund.

110

INDEX

diversification of, 23
management of, 23, 46, 48
prices of, 19–23, 31, 49, 60, 62
selection of, 22, 25
Credit unions, 5, 7
Custodian banks, fees charged by,
15, 25, 51

Deficit financing, 77
Disability insurance, 54
Discount brokers, 51
Distribution
lump-sum, 64
lump-sum vs. installment, 85–87
premature, 69
Diversification, 61–62, 75
method of, 63–64
in mutual funds, 24, 63
Dividend yields, 30–31, 34–35
Dollar, value of, 88
Donoghue's *Money Fund Directory*,
16
Donoghue's *Money Fund Report*, 16
Dow Jones Industrial Average, 31

Economic booms, 20, 22, 42
Economic growth, 19
Economic Recovery Tax Act (1981),
ix

"Family of funds." *See* fund
groups
Federal Deposit Insurance
Corporation (FDIC), 6–7, 41
Federal Savings and Loan
Insurance Corporation
(FSLIC), 6–7
Fees
of banks, 6
of brokerage firms, 45–46, 50–52
of common stock funds, 24–25
of custodian banks, 15, 25, 51
of insurance companies, 53, 55
of money market funds, 10, 15
for switching sponsors, 64
see also commissions
Fidelity bond insurance, 14
Forbes, 29–30

Form 1040, xii, 69
Form 1040A, xii
Form 5329, 69
Form W–4, xiv
Fund groups, 15, 24, 63
Fund managers
reliability of, 25–26
taxation problems of, 35–36
Futures trading, 47

Gas securities, 50
Gold, 37–38, 42–44, 76
Goldbugs, 42
Growth Fund Guide, 29
Growth-income funds, 26–27
"Growth stocks," 20

Income funds, 26–27
Income tax. *See* tax, taxation
Individual Retirement Accounts
(IRAs)
advertising for, 4, 15, 18, 51,
79–80
contributions to, xi–xii, 62–63,
87, 89–92
defined, ix
double tax advantage of, 90
eligibility for, xi
employer-sponsored, 55,
100–102
flexibility of, 4, 9, 14–15, 45, 52,
54–55, 62, 70, 73
insurance on, 7
questions to ask about, 4–5,
59–60, 106–110
self–directed, 45
Simplified Employee Pension,
103
spousal, xiii, 92
Individual retirement annuity, 54
Inflation, 14, 15, 37, 73–78
bank investments and, 5
bonds and, 38–39, 74
causes of, 77
compensation for, 6, 73–74
dollar value and, 88
gold and, 38, 42–44, 75
IRA as hedge against, xi, 44

112